Contents

Open Gate, 61" x 83", 1999. Photo by Peter West

Preface

THIS BOOK IS FOR YOU!

This is a teaching, learning, and exploring book. It is ideal for the beginner who wants to learn about reverse appliqué and the needle-turn method, and it is perfect for the more experienced sewer who wishes to develop appliqué skills in a different and inspirational way.

- The Beginner's Workshop in Reverse Appliqué (page 20) follows a workshop format, using a small sample to take you step-by-step, by text and illustration, through the reverse appliqué method and needle-turn technique.
- Basic skills can be learned and developed through a range of appealing projects that gradually increase in degree of difficulty.
- The projects explore a variety of ideas that have been inspired by metalwork, with alternative approaches suggested where appropriate.
- You can make the principal project, *The Garden Gate* quilt, by using the pullout pattern at the back of the book. Or, if you prefer to be more original, inspirational illustrations and simple directions are available for creating your own picture and designing your own gate.

"DILYS THE QUILT"

"Why don't you come along and have a go?" These immortal words, casually addressed to me in 1983 when I was living in Dorset (a county in southern England), should have carried a government health warning! I was attending a local craft show, minding my own business, when an appliqué quilt made by Jenny Dove, a teacher, came into my line of vision. I had never seen anything like it before and was drawn to it. I savored the overall effect of the quilt—the impact of colors, the combination of fabrics, the delicacy of design, and the texture of the quilting. I accepted an invitation to a workshop, made an appliquéd pillow front, and from that moment I found where I wanted to be, without realizing that I had been searching for somewhere to go!

It is worth adding that I was a total non-sewer. Although my mother was a competent embroiderer, I had no history of a life surrounded by fabric. I directed the considerable enthusiasms and energies of my youth to participating in sports, and I would no more have picked up a needle than flown to the moon.

One pillow front later, I signed up for adult education classes. Any normal person would have embarked on a second pillow, but I launched

To Roger, who keeps me smiling

Big warm-hearted thanks to all my "friends in stitches" who contributed to this book and picked up a needle when time became tight: Dot Aellen, Jean Anderson, Loretta Bailey, Carol Clee, Jennifer Ellis, Connie Evans, Audrey Foster, Mary Greenwood, Jane Hadfield, Jan Huxley, Jan Jones, Lesley Kendall, Barbara Lane, Kath Lloyd, Janet Parry, Liz Pedley, Barbara Platt, Margaret Robson, Julie Scoffield, Mair Scott, Pip Sumbler, Barbara Thomas, Mary Williams, Denise Willis, and Sylvia Wood. Thanks to Brian Pollard for the extensive photography and his calm commitment to completing it in time.

Thanks to my special friend Judy Dales, who gave wise counsel and encouragement during the preparation of the manuscript.

Thanks to my new friends at C&T: Cyndy Rymer, Diane Pedersen, Sara MacFarland, Tim Manibusan, and Aliza Shalit, who helped me feel like one of the team in spite of the miles between us.

straight into a king-size quilt, with twenty appliquéd blocks and wide, quilted borders. I dipped into Jenny's pattern box each week and worked with blind confidence and unrelenting enthusiasm, while enjoying the variety of projects done by other students. Apart from the obvious benefits of belonging to a group that shared a similar passion, where else could you go to fondle fabrics and drool over books without being arrested? But it wasn't all smooth sailing. Not being a natural sewer, I had to learn the hard way. For example, when Jenny told me that the way to get flat appliqué was to keep my fabrics as flat as possible, I took her literally, and I sewed my appliqué flat on a tabletop. I still do it this way. Also, I wasn't aware that there is a difference between appliqué and patchwork: the patchwork blocks on that first quilt are squares and triangles appliquéd onto the background! I cobbled this quilt together, quilted with real "toe catcher" stitches (four-to-the-inch), and showed it off with immense pride. Faded, flat, limp, and worn it may now be, but it represents my awakening.

Until that time, I did not realize that I possessed a creative bone in my body or a feel for color and an aptitude for design. My first quilt opened the doors to awareness and gave me confidence to sew my way into a fascinating and diverse craft. Now, my favorite expression is "I feel a quilt coming on!" I just can't help myself.

The moral of my introduction to my quiltmaking story is that if I can do it, anyone can. During the last eighteen years, I have sewn whenever possible, taught extensively, written periodically, and never tired of it. I have continued to learn through teaching, increased my expertise in all aspects of quiltmaking, tried new ideas, made mistakes, and tried again. I am still thirsty for more. There is a quaint tradition in Wales that tradespeople are often known locally as "Jones the Post," "Thomas the Milk," and so on. Since living in North Wales where I have become acquainted with others who share the Welsh name of Dilys, I am sometimes distinguished from them as "Dilys the Quilt," a label I wear with pride.

Join me on my latest journey into reverse appliqué. Learning the hard way has made me a sympathetic teacher; I hope this will be evident throughout the book. You will learn through workshop samples, with lots of visual references. Interesting and varied projects of increasing levels of difficulty will help you develop your technique. The final quilt, *The Garden Gate*, is designed to let you show off your reverse appliqué skills.

All in Vane (detail), 74" x 98", 1993. Machine pieced and appliquéd; machine and hand quilted.

Escherflies, 49" x 56", 1995. Hand reverse appliquéd, and machine and hand quilted.

Introduction

Time has passed creatively since my introduction to quiltmaking in 1983. The quilts shown here are the ones that are relevant to the development of the techniques used in this book.

My fascination with weather vanes began during a family boating holiday on the Norfolk Broads. When I found there was a traditional "weather vane" block, it seemed logical to team this up with the images of vanes that I had collected. There is no reverse appliqué in *All in Vane*, but it is the first time I used the idea of silhouetting with black fabric.

Cutwork embroidery inspired the flower motifs in *Taking Liberties with Cutwork*. A circular quilting pattern and a feather-and-rope border were adapted to look like stencils for reverse appliqué. Liberty fabrics in a value sequence give a feeling of shading in the outer border.

Inspired by an M.C. Escher design, *Escherflies* features reverse appliqué. The background fabrics for the colorwash and the butterfly wings were created first, before being placed behind the black foreground fabric. The black and white border was constructed using a paper foundation for accuracy.

The starting point for *Overwrought I* was a circular motif on a balcony in France. Common wrought-iron designs and grids were drafted to continue the theme of this quilt, and wrought-iron scrolls were featured as quilting designs, sewing them with a contrasting thread.

A collection of wrought-iron and cast-iron designs was the inspiration for *Overwrought II*. I planned the layout on graph paper, designing it to combine a foreground "fabric" that is actually three colors of the same fabric. Then I drafted the patterns to size and sewed them shape by shape before combining them into the quilt.

The variety in the work shown here illustrates that the journey along my creative pathway has been unpredictable. The evidence shows that I have been sampling techniques, testing methods, fine-tuning my skills, establishing my preferences, and always working in a creative fashion. This unconscious process has helped to establish in my mind what I enjoy doing and how I prefer to do it, until eventually I arrived at the garden gate.

Taking Liberties with Cutwork, 48" x 65", 1994. Hand reverse appliquéd and hand quilted

Overwrought II, 53" x 85", 1992. Hand reverse appliquéd and hand quilted

Overwrought I, 54" x 54", 1990. Hand reverse appliquéd and quilted

Ironwork as a Decorative Element

EXAMPLES OF ANTIQUE WROUGHT IRON

Considered the most useful of metals, iron has been a decorative element in architecture for over a thousand years. Its uses range from decorating flat surfaces like doors and locks to making freestanding structures such as gates and railings. As wrought iron, shaped in a forge by a blacksmith, it is malleable, robust, and shock resistant, providing both strength in its form and delicacy in its decoration. In contrast, cast iron is produced in a foundry and pressed into molds, allowing for the mass production of identical forms.

Early examples of decorative ironwork include hinges, lock plates, firedogs (andirons), firebacks, candlesticks, church grilles, brackets, gates, hinges, and railings. Unlike the metalwork used to decorate the wood on church doors, open ironwork gates, railings, and grilles were constructed to form transparent barriers that both guarded and revealed the beauty beyond.

In wrought iron all design possibilities are based on a linear structure. The initial stage in the construction process is to provide a strong and stable framework that is filled in with decorative scrollwork.

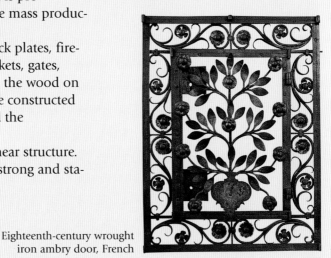

Eighteenth-century wrought iron balcony, French

Eighteenth-century wrought iron ambry door, French

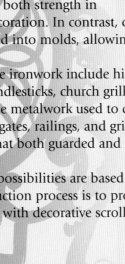

Eighteenth-century wrought-iron balusters from staircases, English

Sixteenth-century window grating, German

All photos this page courtesy of the Victoria & Albert Museum, London.

EXAMPLES OF MODERN WROUGHT IRON

London balcony

Gates to Eaton Hall

Piccadilly railings

London window grille

Detail from the White Gates of Leeswood.
Photo by Brian Pollard

Red gate

Heart and honeysuckle balcony

The clock tower in
Chester. Photo by
Roger C. Fronks

Photos by the author with noted exceptions.

CHAPTER TWO

Sewing Essentials

The first part of this chapter lists supplies needed to create the projects. The following section explains and illustrates the skills required to help you make the "Taster" block in the reverse appliqué workshop. Concise instructions and clear illustrations, plus useful tips, make the process easy to understand. Good advice is offered for coping with concave and convex curves, and for inward and outward points. My tabletop method of sewing is explained, with details of the advantages of sewing this way.

The second part of this chapter details the techniques required to construct and finish the projects shown in the book, offering helpful advice on many skills, including adding straight and mitered borders, prairie points, bindings, and so on.

Supplies

The basic supplies for the projects in this book are readily available to all quilters. I believe the process of sewing should be kept simple and uncluttered. The emphasis should be on the fabrics, and the sewing methods that will ultimately give the desired results. Pioneer women made some wonderful appliqué quilts with very few supplies to distract them. They made do with what was on hand.

Basic supplies

Ballpoint pen: Use with dressmaker's carbon paper to transfer the pattern onto the fabric because the metal tip produces a clear line and the pen can be held efficiently to provide prolonged pressure. A dried-up ballpoint pen provides the necessary pressure without marking the pattern.

Basic sewing supplies: Straight pins, safety pins, sewing needles, and a thimble (optional).

Batting: A good quality cotton batting stabilizes the fabric during quilting and assists with the drape of a wall quilt.

Cutting mat, rotary cutter, and ruler: Use specifically for preparing the squares for the garden picture; also helpful for squaring the edges of pillows, wallhangings, and quilts.

Design wall: An essential part of the picture "painting" process, this can range from a portable, rigid board to a large wall covered with any material with a fluffy surface that will grip and hold the fabric squares without pinning.

Drafting supplies: Graph paper, ruler, pencil, compass, tracing paper, and template plastic.

Dressmaker's carbon paper: Recommended for transferring the pattern lines onto dark fabric. Choose the white and yellow sheets to produce good, clear lines that remain visible during the sometimes lengthy hand-sewing process.

Fabric: Use lightweight, good quality cotton fabrics, prewashed at your own discretion.

Masking tape: Use to secure the pattern and fabric on a flat surface.

Scissors: Small scissors with sharp points for clipping seam allowances and cutting between the layers.

Sewing machine in good working order: To sew $1/4$" seams during the construction of the watercolor picture, for optional machine quilting and zigzag stitching, and for assembling the projects.

Thread: For hand sewing, use cotton threads that closely match the foreground fabrics; for machine construction use neutral threads. You will also need basting and hand or machine quilting thread.

Stitching Basics

FABRIC GRAIN

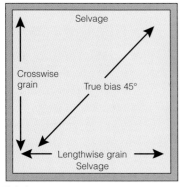

Fabric terms

NEEDLE-TURN APPLIQUÉ

This method of sewing is ideal for appliqué, as well as reverse appliqué because it results in accurately turned edges. Preparation is minimal, requiring only the transfer of a master pattern onto fabric, a small amount of basting, and no templates. As the name suggests, you use the needle for turning under the seam allowance before sewing it down. With practice, the needle becomes a valuable tool for maneuvering the seam allowance and maintaining the edge of the shape by adjusting it to the marked line. In both appliqué and reverse appliqué, you can rely on the same techniques to handle concave and convex curves, outward points, and inward V shapes.

Being right-handed, I always sew counterclockwise (from right to left) around the outer edge of an appliqué shape. When sewing a reverse appliqué cutout, I still sew from right to left but the direction becomes clockwise because the inside edge of the shape is being sewn. I work with the marked line closer to me than the cut edge of the fabric. I find it more comfortable to "sweep" the seam toward me rather than to push it away. It is easier to control the stitch and to position the needle to catch the edge of the shape.

The Appliqué Stitch

Thread a needle with thread that closely matches the foreground fabric, remembering that the smaller the needle, the better the control. Put a small knot in one cut end to provide a firm anchor. Hide the knot under the marked line by bringing the needle up through the foreground fabric on the inside edge of the marked line.

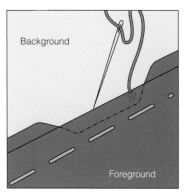

Anchor the knot under the folded edge.

TIP: Where possible, start to sew on a straight line or gentle curve. Do not start at a point.

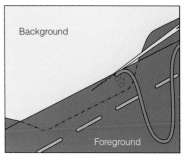

Insert the needle parallel to the edge and take a small stitch.

The needle should go straight down into the background fabric and slightly underneath the edge of the shape.

TIP: Do not travel forward as you go down into the background fabric; this makes a longer stitch that is likely to be visible.

TIP: Inserting the needle slightly underneath the shape, rather than in line with the edge, allows the thread to blend in better on the edge, concealing the stitch.

TIP: Do not travel forward more than $1/8$". Gaps in the stitches allow the seam allowance to slip, resulting in corners on curves and loose ends on points.

Pull the sewing thread firmly to tighten the stitch but not so tightly as to cause puckering.

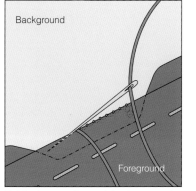

Guide the needle straight down, and travel forward underneath, catching a few threads on the folded edge.

Continue sewing by reinserting your needle into the background in the same place it came out. The traveling must always take place underneath the background fabric.

TIP: *Test the seam by pulling at the edge of the appliqué shape. If you can see the stitches along the edge, you are either traveling too far forward with each stitch or not pulling your thread tight enough.*

Sewing the Curves

There are two types of curves—concave and convex–and they may range from gentle bends in a line to tight inward or outward circles.

A **concave** curve "caves" or bows inward. With this curve, there will be less fabric at the cut edge of the seam allowance than at the marked edge of the shape. Clipping is necessary to allow the seam allowance to stretch as it is turned under.

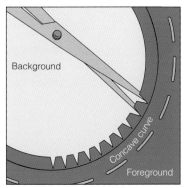

Clip three-quarters of the way into the seam allowance on concave curves.

TIP: *As a general rule, the sharper the curve, the closer together the clips should be. If the curve is severe, snip clips as close together as $^1/_8$".*

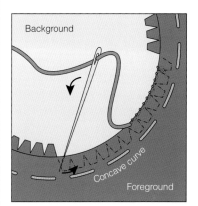

Use the needle to sweep under the seam allowance.

Sew small, close stitches to secure the edge to the background fabric and maintain the curve.

A **convex** curve bows outward. With this curve, there will be more fabric at the cut edge of the seam allowance than at the marked edge of the shape. In this instance, use the needle to rearrange the seam allowance so it lies flat under the edge of the shape. These curves are often only as good as the marked line; transfer the pattern onto the fabric carefully.

TIP: *Do not clip into the seam allowances on convex curves because this may encourage "corners" to appear on the sewn edge.*

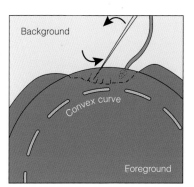

Sweep the seam allowance under to the marked line.

Using the tip of the needle, turn under and even out the seam allowance. Sew the edge of the shape down with small, close stitches to prevent the seam allowance from escaping. Turn and hold down only a small portion of the seam allowance at any one time, and sew a couple of close stitches before readjusting the seam to the marked line. On the edge of a circle, particularly a small one, take only one stitch at a time before readjusting.

TIP: *Close stitching and constant readjustment to the line result in smooth convex curves.*

If you turn under too much seam allowance, distorting the edge of the shape, use the needle under the fold to ease the edge out to the marked line again.

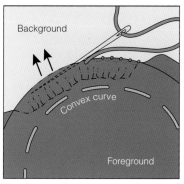

Use the needle to ease the shape to the marked line.

Sewing the Outward Points

Outward points can vary from a gently angled corner to the sharpest of elongated points. Gentle points are easy to shape by sewing an extra stitch on the corner to hold the point. As the point sharpens, the space where the fabric has to be folded becomes smaller. For that reason you may need to trim some of the excess fabric.

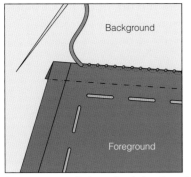

As you approach the point, bring the stitches closer together and sew right to the tip.

Rotate the background fabric so the seam on the point lies to the side.

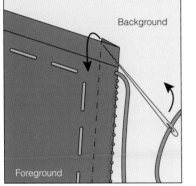

Pick up both seam allowances near the fold and sweep them under.

Sweep the point of the needle toward yourself, so the seam allowances fold under the shape and lie snug against the stitched edge. Holding the point down, again tug on the stitch at the point to sharpen it. Sew close stitches on the other side of the point to hold under the seam allowance.

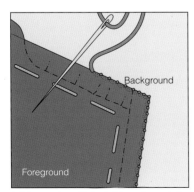

Add an extra stitch right on the point. Sew away from the point.

If the point is elongated and there is too much fabric in the seam allowance to hide underneath the shape, reduce the fabric bulk. Anchor the point as before, then fold back the appliqué shape to reveal the seam allowance under the point. Using sharp scissors, cut parallel to the direction of the point, trimming away a small amount of the fabric in the seam allowance. Turn under the remaining seam allowance, hold down the fabric on the point, and use the needle to readjust the seam allowance so it lies flat. Sew away from the point with close stitches as before.

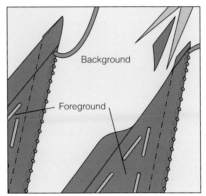

On an elongated point, fold the appliqué shape back and trim away the excess fabric from the seam allowance.

Sewing the Inward V Shapes

TIP: *At the point of the V, the seam allowances go in opposite directions, leaving no fabric to turn under. Because the stitches here will always be visible, a good match of thread with fabric is important.*

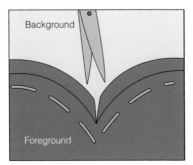

Clip to the marked line at the V, but do *not* cut through the line.

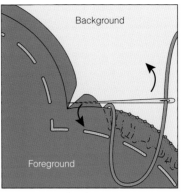

Sweep the seam allowance under with the needle. Sew with close stitches to maintain the shape.

As you approach the V, bring the stitches on the turned edge closer together—approximately ⅛" apart. Sew to within ⅛" of the inward point, taking care to avoid fraying the edge. Insert the needle down into the background fabric as if you were making a stitch, but bring it up about ⅛" below the marked point of the V.

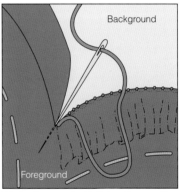

Stitch close to the V. Bring the needle up deep in the V.

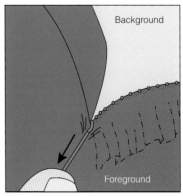

Take a stitch through the foreground fabric only, and pull it deep into the V.

Pull tight on this stitch and take a second stitch deep in the V, through the background fabric, securing the shape in place. Rotate the shape, turn the seam allowance under on the other side of the V, and sew away from the V.

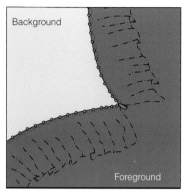

Put a second stitch into the background to hold the exaggerated V, and sew away from the V with close stitches.

THE TABLETOP METHOD

My tabletop sewing procedure began as a misunderstanding between my teacher and I. Not being a natural sewer, I had to learn the hard way as I initially struggled for results and eventually for excellence. My teacher told her students that our goal was to produce flat appliqué. To do this, we had to keep our fabrics as flat as possible while we were sewing them. I took her literally and started to sew, trying to keep my fabrics flat on the table. Although this initially proved awkward and often frustrating, I persevered until it became second nature. If you wish to try this method, remember that it gets easier with practice!

There are several advantages to the tabletop method.

1. The fabrics remain flat and do not move in relation to one another. There is none of the distortion that sometimes occurs when your fingers are underneath the fabrics.

Sewing flat on a tabletop

2. The table supports your elbows, eliminating strain in the upper arm and neck region. A tilted board underneath the work area stops you from hunching over your work.

Sewing on a tilted board

3. The design is often seen more fully in front of you than when you sew in your lap, making it easier to see the shapes in relation to each other and to assess your progress during sewing.

4. Although most of the sewing occurs alongside the index finger, you can hold down longer sections of seam allowance using the rest of your fingers on top of the work.

5. Extensive basting is unnecessary, which must be an advantage! I often use small safety pins in my work, eliminating basting altogether.

6. This technique is adaptable to any room in your home: place a tray across the arms of a chair to create a work surface at a comfortable height, and add a daylight bulb to a well-placed lamp for good lighting.

TIP: *As a recent development, I now quilt my background patchwork gardens first, before overlaying them with a gate pattern. Working flat, I baste with pins and sew comfortably at a table without having to put my left hand underneath to support the fabrics or grip a bulky quilt.*

Sewing Using the Tabletop Method

The right hand controls the needle, and the left hand is placed on top of the work with the fingers along the edge of the line to be sewn. (Reverse this arrangement if you are left-handed.)

The thumb and forefinger of the right hand direct the needle into the fabric. The middle finger, thimbled for protection if preferred, pushes the needle through, to be collected again by the thumb and forefinger.

The fingers of the left hand act as a buffer at the edge of the shape. As the needle negotiates the fabric, the fingers prevent the edge from slipping. The edge of the shape is pushed against the index finger, allowing the needle to catch the underside of the fold on its way up again.

Basic Techniques

PREPARING A MASTER PATTERN

Because book pages are limited in size, it is sometimes necessary to prepare a Master Pattern before starting a project. This is particularly true of reverse appliqué projects, which are not template based. You need a complete pattern to transfer onto the foreground fabric.

Cut the paper to the size of the piece of work stated in the pattern, and draw vertical and horizontal centerlines.

Make multiple tracings or photocopies of the pattern sections to the required size. Tape them to the paper, being aware of the centerlines.

ADDING A SEAM INSERT

To define a seam or emphasize a border strip, add a small, folded insert of contrasting fabric before sewing on the border strips. Cut the contrasting fabric $3/4$"-wide and the length of the edge. Fold it in half, wrong sides together, and press. With all raw edges even, baste the strip in place using a $1/8$" seam allowance and matching thread. When you sew the border with a $1/4$" seam, you will see $1/8$" of the insert.

Press, wrong sides together, and baste in place.

ADDING STRAIGHT BORDERS

Measure the size of the square (for example, $12^1/_2$") and decide on the width of the border strips (for example, $3^1/_2$", which results in an $18^1/_2$" square). Cut the top and bottom border strips as long as the top edge of the square ($12^1/_2$") and as wide as the border ($3^1/_2$"). Using a $1/4$" seam, sew these in place, and press both seam allowances toward the border.

Measure the center square from top to bottom, including the borders ($18^1/_2$"). Cut the strips this long and as wide as the border (or $3^1/_2$" x $18^1/_2$"). Sew them to the sides of the square. Press the seams toward the border.

ADDING MITERED BORDERS

Measure the size of the square (for example, $14^1/_2$") and decide on the width of the border strips (for example, $2^1/_2$", which results in an $18^1/_2$" square). Cut the strips long enough to allow the fabrics to overlap comfortably on the corners ($19^1/_2$" x $2^1/_2$"). Using pins, mark the center of each side of the square and the center of each border strip. Matching the center points, pin the borders to the square, right sides together and raw edges even. An equal amount of border fabric will extend beyond each corner.

Starting and stopping $1/4$" from the corners, sew each of the borders to the square. Backstitch to make the corners secure, and remove the pins. Press the seams toward the outside edge.

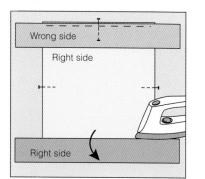

Center the strip, start sewing $1/4$" from one corner, and finish $1/4$" from the next corner.

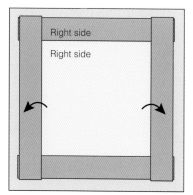

Add the side borders in the same way, leaving the corners free.

Carefully fold the center square diagonally, right sides together, lining up the border strips at the corners. Pin the strips to prevent them from slipping.

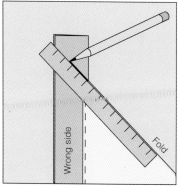

Fold the center square on the diagonal, and extend the diagonal line onto the border strips by drawing or creasing against the ruler.

Sew on this marked line by hand or machine, starting from the point on the corner where the previous stitches stopped. Trim away the excess fabric, leaving $1/4$" seam allowance. Repeat the procedure for each corner.

Press the seams open.

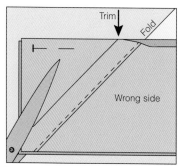

Pin and sew along the marked line, trim the excess fabric.

MAKING CONTINUOUS PRAIRIE POINTS

Each prairie point will finish equal in size to one-quarter of the width of the fabric strip from which it is cut. For example, the points will be 2" if you cut them from an 8"-wide strip.

Cut a strip of fabric the required width (for example, 6"), and press it in half along its length, wrong sides together. Open it again, and lay it on a flat surface, wrong side up, for marking and cutting. Mark the centerline in the fold. Measure and mark each side of the center-line, dividing each section into staggered or offset squares (for example, 3"). In other words, the corner of a square on one side will lie midway between the corners of a square on the other side. Trim the unwanted half-square (for example, 3" x 1$\frac{1}{2}$") at the beginning and end of each staggered line.

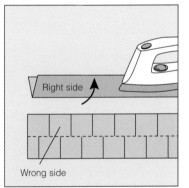
Mark and cut into sections, staggering one side against the other.

Cut along these marked lines from the raw edge to the fold along the entire length of the strip. Press each square in half on the diagonal, making triangles.

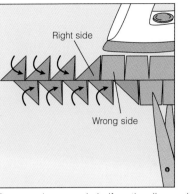
Press each square in half on the diagonal, making triangles.

Fold each triangle in half again, making it smaller. The raw edges should meet along the fold of the strip. Fold the strip in half again lengthwise, tucking the prairie points together, and press.

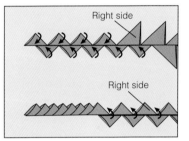
Press in half again. Fold the two sides together. Tuck one point into the next, and baste $\frac{1}{8}$" from the folded edge.

MAKING AN OVERLAPPED PILLOW BACK

Measure the front of the pillow (for example, 18"), and cut out one piece that is the same width and half the length plus 1" for a seam allowance (18" x 10"). Turn under the seam allowance (so it measures 18" x 9"), and lay the piece, wrong side up, on a flat surface.

Cut another piece that measures the width of the pillow and half the length plus 5" (for example, 18" x 14"). Turn under the seam allowance (so it measures 18" x 13"), and place and pin the pillow back wrong side up on top of the first piece, making a square the same size as the pillow front (for example, 18"). Place the pillow front, right side up, on top, matching the raw edges. The pillow is now ready for binding.

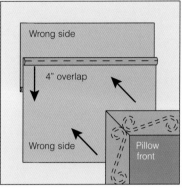
Make a second piece that is 5" longer. Lay one piece on top of the other to fit the pillow front.

MAKING A ZIPPERED PILLOW BACK

Measure the front of the pillow (for example, 16"), and cut a square of fabric which is 2" larger (18"). Cut the fabric square in half (18" x 9"). On the wrong side of one half draw a line 1" away from one cut edge.

Tidy the raw edges, and baste the pieces, right sides together along the marked line.

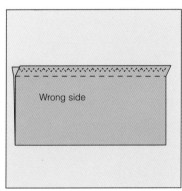
Baste pieces right sides together.

Use a zipper that is 1" shorter than the pillow front (15"). Baste the zipper over the seam.

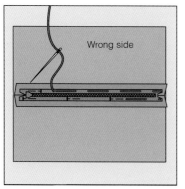

On the wrong side, baste the zipper over the seam. Sew close to the teeth.

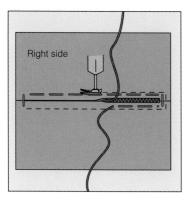

On the right side, sew outside of the basting stitches, and remove basting stitches to reveal the zipper.

Position the prepared pillow back right side down on a flat surface, and place the pillow front on top, right side up and centered. Trim the excess fabric to even the edges. The pillow is ready for binding (page 18).

USING SEE-THROUGH RULERS

The large, see-through rulers that you use with a rotary cutter and cutting board are invaluable in the finishing-off process. Because they are transparent, you can line up the vertical and horizontal lines on the ruler with the seams in your quilt to make right-angle corners. Use the diagonal 45° lines to mark quilting lines.

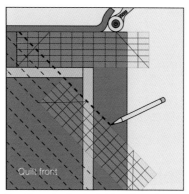

Use the ruler to straighten the edges and mark 45° lines for quilting.

PREPARING FOR QUILTING

In addition to holding the layers of the quilt together, quilting adds texture to your overall design. Quilting close to an appliquéd edge allows the shape to fill out; lines of quilting repeated around shapes, or echo quilting, help to emphasize shapes. Patterns and grids on the background help to unify the different blocks in a quilt.

Press the quilt top and remove loose threads from the back. This is particularly important if you are using a light fabric; "ghosts" of loose threads can appear and will be difficult to remove after quilting. Place the top right side up onto the batting and backing, both of which should be cut slightly larger (in case of movement during quilting). Pin the quilt layers together before thread-basting in horizontal and vertical rows spaced about 3-4" apart. For machine quilting, use safety pins rather than basting with thread.

TRANSFERRING PATTERN LINES FOR QUILTING

A marked line needs to be obvious during the quilting process, but it needs to disappear into the line of stitches once it has been sewn. The easiest way to transfer a pattern onto fabric is to trace it, but this is impossible with dark fabrics unless you use a light box. Dressmaker's carbon is unsuitable because the line is too obvious. A tried and tested way to create an acceptable line is to make a template of the shape and draw around it with an appropriate marker, creating a thin, visible line for hand or machine quilting.

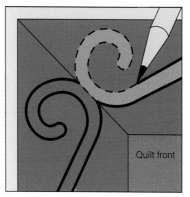

Draw around the template with a suitable marker.

A recommended way for transferring a pattern for quilting using the sewing machine is to trace the pattern onto good-quality tissue paper. Pin it on the fabric, and machine quilt along the pattern lines using a short stitch and thread that contrasts with the fabric. The paper is easy to remove because the needle perforates it as it sews. Use this method to transfer a pattern line onto background fabric for the stained-glass technique (page 50) when it is impossible to trace.

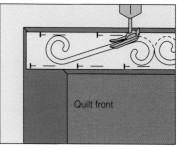

Trace the pattern onto tissue paper, and sew through it using the machine.

EXAMPLES OF TEXTURAL MACHINE QUILTING

Samples of textured machine quilting

Whatever you can draw with a pencil, you should be able to draw with a machine needle, too! An acquired skill, free-motion machine quilting is useful when quilting a large quilt, the main advantage being that there is no need to rotate the quilt. You need a good grip on the quilt for extra

control. Aim, too, for steady coordination of the sewing speed, regulated by your foot, and the stitch length, controlled by your hand. I leave my feed dogs up for a bit of extra grip on the underside of the quilt. Remember that practice makes perfect.

ATTACHING A HANGING SLEEVE

I automatically attach a hanging sleeve to the back of my quilts and wallhangings, using backing fabric to conceal the sleeve.

Cut a strip of backing fabric 4" wide and 1" shorter than the measurement of the top edge of the quilt. Turn under and sew a small seam on each of the short edges, and iron under a $1/4$" seam along one long edge. Pin the sleeve onto the back of the quilt, raw edges even. Sew it in place when binding the edge. Sew the lower edge to the backing layer by hand, using matching thread and concealed stitches.

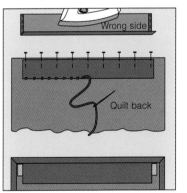

Tidy the short edges, and pin the sleeve to the top back of the quilt. Sew it into the binding. Hand sew the lower edge.

If you prefer, you may protect the back of your quilt by using a double sleeve: Cut fabric 8" wide and 1" shorter than the top edge. Narrowly hem the short edges, and

fold the fabric in half, wrong sides together. Catch the long, raw edges in the seam when binding the top edge of the quilt. Sew the folded edge of the sleeve to the backing fabric by hand.

DOUBLE-FOLD BINDING

Preparing a Binding Strip

Measure around the outside edge of the quilt or pillow front. On the straight grain of the fabric, cut enough 2"-wide strips to exceed this measurement by about 10". Stitch these strips together to make a single piece long enough to travel all the way around the edge. A diagonal (bias) seam is better than a straight one because it adds less bulk to the seam. To join, place two strips, right sides together, at right angles to one another. Sew at a 45° angle, and cut away the excess fabric on the corner, leaving a $1/4$" seam allowance. Iron the seam open, and fold the strip in half along its length, wrong sides together.

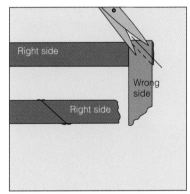

Place the strips at right angles, right sides together. Sew at a 45° angle, and cut off the corner. Press the seam open.

Cut the starting edge of the binding at a 45° angle to tidy the edge, turn and press a $1/4$" seam allowance.

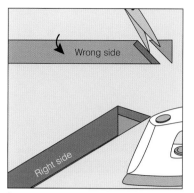

Start the strip at an angle, with a pressed seam allowance.

Binding the Edges

Make sure that your binding strip is long enough to go all the way around the edge, adding an extra 10" to allow for mitered corners and an overlap at the ends.

Place the start of the binding strip about 3" from a corner, matching the raw edges of the strip with those of the pillow or quilt. Leaving about 2" at the start for the overlap, sew on the binding with a $\frac{1}{4}$" seam. Stop sewing $\frac{1}{4}$" from the corner, and backstitch to secure the stitches. Remove from under the sewing foot.

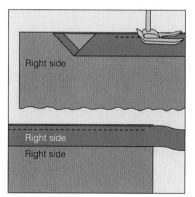

Start sewing 2" from end of binding and stop sewing $\frac{1}{4}$" from the next corner.

At the corner, you make a tuck by pulling the binding up at a 90° angle away from you, and then toward you again. The fold of the tuck must be level with the raw edges of the pillow or quilt. If the tuck is too low, the corner will be squashed; if the tuck is too high, the corner will be elongated. Insert the corner under the sewing foot, and, from the top of the tuck, resume sewing a $\frac{1}{4}$" seam.

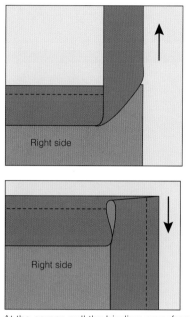

At the corner, pull the binding away from you and then fold toward you to make a tuck.

After sewing the final corner, trim the end of the binding at an angle, and overlap it with the starting edge by $\frac{1}{2}$". Slide it inside the start of the strip. Sew to complete the seam. Turn the folded edge of the binding onto the back of the quilt. Sew it down by hand using matching thread and concealed stitches, mitering the extra fabric on the corners. Hand sew the overlap seam.

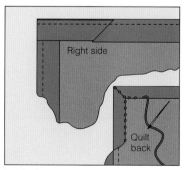

Angle the end, and insert it into the start. On the back, sew the folded strip by hand.

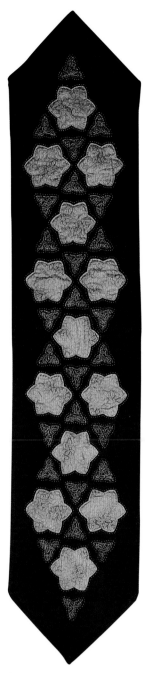

Christmas Bellpull (pattern 3, using two background fabrics), Barbara Platt, Ellesmere, Shropshire, England, 2001

Beginner's Workshop in Reverse Appliqué

This section is presented in a workshop format to take you step by step through each stage of the reverse appliqué method. It includes a simple cast-iron design as a "Taster" block that incorporates inward and outward curves and points. Use this pattern to learn and practice the reverse appliqué method, working along with the text and referring to the illustrations. The project is small, so you can keep it on file for future reference or finish it off as suggested at the end of the workshop.

TIP: *Get into the habit of reading each set of instructions through before beginning a project so there are no surprises ahead.*

Familiarize yourself with the fabric terms on page 11 and be aware of the following terminology:

Foreground refers to the top fabric onto which the pattern is transferred and from which the pattern shapes are cut.

Background refers to the fabrics placed underneath that become visible through the cut pattern shapes in the foreground fabric.

WORKSHOP TASTER BLOCK SAMPLE ONE

Reverse appliqué using one background fabric

FABRIC REQUIREMENTS

Foreground: $9\frac{1}{2}$" square of dark fabric (solid or tone-on-tone)
Background: 8" square of light, contrasting fabric
Other supplies:
 Thread that closely matches the foreground fabric
 Dressmaker's carbon paper
 Dried-up ballpoint pen
 Basic sewing supplies

Reverse appliqué using one background fabric

Transferring the Pattern onto the Fabric

TIP: *Be aware that the sewn shape will be only as good as the marked line when you use the needle-turn method. Take time to transfer an accurate, clear line onto the foreground fabric.*

1. Trace or photocopy the Master Pattern (page 23), marking the centering lines. Find the centerlines of the foreground square by folding it in half vertically and horizontally and finger-pressing along the folds. Use basting thread to sew a line of stitches along these folds.

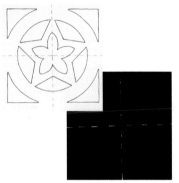

Sew basting stitches along the fold lines.

TIP: *If you press with an iron, the centerlines will be too pronounced and often difficult to remove.*

2. Place the prepared foreground fabric onto a flat surface with the right side up, and hold it in place using masking tape. Place the Master Pattern on top of the right side of the fabric, matching the centerlines of the pattern with those of the fabric. Hold it in place with pins or masking tape placed along the top edge only, outside the marked pattern.

Center the pattern on the fabric.

TIP: *Use masking tape instead of pins for a flatter effect.*

3. Test the carbon paper to make sure it transfers onto your fabric. Carefully lift the lower edge of the pattern, and slide the carbon paper underneath, colored side down, onto the foreground fabric. Secure the lower edge using pins or masking tape.

Slide the carbon paper between the pattern and fabric, colored side down.

4. Systematically transfer all the pattern lines onto the fabric using a ballpoint pen, and a ruler where necessary. Be aware that you are marking an area that will be cut out; try to mark along the inside edge of the pattern line. Before removing the pattern and carbon paper from the fabric, check to see that you have transferred all the pattern lines.

Transfer the pattern onto the fabric.

TIP: *Study the pattern to see which shapes should be cut away and which will remain. You may find it helpful at this stage to snip a small cut in the center of each of the shapes to be cut away. This will make it easier to get the point of the scissors into the foreground fabric after you have basted the layers together.*

Combining the Foreground and Background

Place the square of background fabric right side up on a flat surface. Place the foreground fabric on top, also right side up, to show the marked lines. Make sure that the background fabric extends $1/2$" beyond the edges of the marked shapes as a "comfort zone." Do this by feel or by holding the squares up to the light to see the shadowing of one against the other. Pin the fabrics together to prepare for basting.

TIP: *In reverse appliqué, as in appliqué, it is important to match the straight grains of both the foreground and background fabrics (page 11) to give stability to the finished sample. To make this easier, get into the habit of cutting squares, strips, and rectangles of the background fabric so you can identify the grain lines easily.*

Place the background fabric underneath the marked foreground fabric.

Basting the Shapes

From the right side, hand baste around every marked shape to hold the fabrics together. Using regular stitches, baste just over $1/4$" outside the marked pattern lines. Try to keep the fabrics flat so there is no movement between the layers. Remove the pins.

Baste outside the marked shapes, $1/4$" outside the line.

Cutting and Clipping

(See page 12 for more information.)

1. Working one shape at a time, cut the fabric away inside the marked pattern line, leaving a $1/4$" seam allowance. Leaving more than $1/4$" may result in excessive bulkiness, particularly on convex curves. As you become more proficient, you can reduce the seam allowance to $3/16$".

2. Clip into the shape where necessary, clipping right up to the marked line on the V shapes and three-quarters of the way into the concave curves. Be aware that the tighter the curves, the closer the clips must be.

Appliquéing the Edge

(See page 11 for more information.)

Needle-turn the edge from the right side.

1. Thread the needle with 18" of thread that closely matches the foreground fabric; knot the end. Bring the needle up through the foreground fabric on the inside edge of the marked line.

2. Pick up the seam allowance using the point of the needle and sweep the needle under the edge of the shape until the marked line is just out of sight. Holding down the turned seam, use the point of the needle to adjust the edge to the marked line if necessary. Sew along the edge of the shape with small, invisible stitches, turning and adjusting the seam allowance as you sew.

3. After sewing all the shapes, remove the basting stitches. Carefully press the sample from the wrong side to settle the stitches and sharpen the edges of the shapes.

Trimming the Back

Reduce the seam allowance from the wrong side.

1. On the wrong side, small stitches define the sewn shapes. Cut away the excess fabric outside of these stitches, creating a seam allowance equal to a scant $1/4$" around each shape.

2. Again, press gently on the wrong side to settle the stitches and sharpen the edges of the shapes.

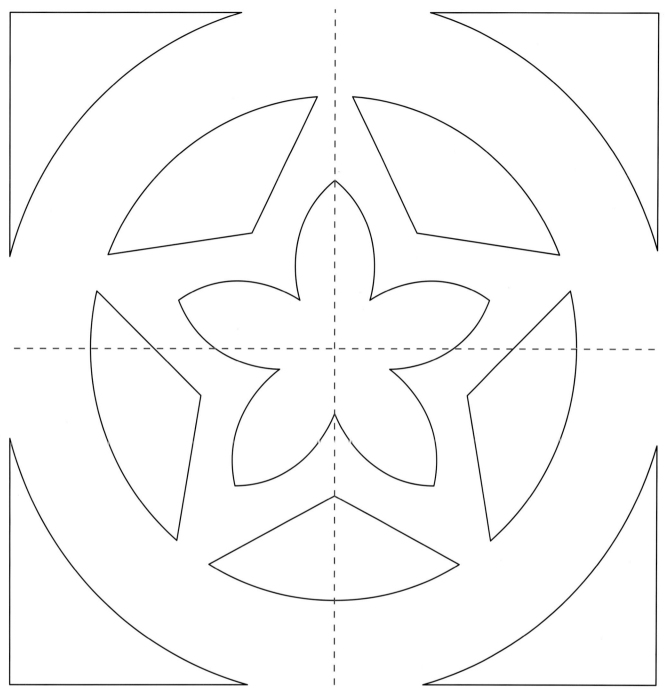

Cast-iron pattern for beginner's workshop

Reverse Appliqué Method in a Nutshell

Step 1. PLACE: Transfer the pattern onto the foreground fabric, and place the background fabric behind the marked shapes in turn.

Step 2. BASTE: Pin and baste $^1/_4$" outside the line marked on the foreground fabric.

Step 3. NEEDLE-TURN: Cut away the fabric inside the marked line to leave a $^3/_{16}$" seam on the outside. Needle-turn and stitch the edge of the foreground fabric to the background fabric.

Step 4. TRIM: From the back, trim away the excess fabric to leave a scant $^1/_4$" seam on the outside of the stitches. Position and sew any other fabrics to complete the design.

SAMPLE TWO

Reverse appliqué using two background fabrics

FABRIC REQUIREMENTS

Foreground: $9^1/_2$" square of dark fabric

Background: 8" square of light floral fabric

Flower: $4^1/_2$" square of bright fabric

Other supplies:

 Thread that closely matches the foreground fabric

 Dressmaker's carbon paper

 Dried-up ballpoint pen

 Basic sewing supplies

Reverse appliqué using two background fabrics

Assembly

1. Following the procedure outlined for Sample One (page 21), transfer the pattern lines onto the right side of the foreground fabric. Place the light background fabric behind, and pin and baste only around the pattern shapes that are to be cut away— the corners and wedges of the first background fabric in the sample. Cut parallel to the marked pattern line, leaving a manageable seam allowance. Clip, turn, and sew one shape at a time (page 12).

2. After sewing the corners and wedges in place, remove the basting stitches and carefully press the sample. From the back, cut away the excess fabric, trimming just outside the stitched shapes, also trimming away the layer of background fabric from behind the flower.

3. Pin and baste the precut square of bright fabric behind the marked flower shape, matching the fabric grain lines. Cut away the foreground fabric, clip the seam allowance, needle-turn the edge, and stitch it in place using small, concealed stitches. Remove the basting stitches, and press the sample. To finish, reduce the seam allowances from the back (page 22).

Reverse appliqué using a directional print

When positioning a directional print or specific motif behind a foreground shape, placement must be accurate and consistent to give a visually pleasing balance to the pattern. To achieve this in reverse appliqué the foreground is cut away before the background fabric is basted securely behind it. Be aware that in this example the straight grains of the background and foreground fabrics will not be parallel, which may cause distortion in a larger piece of work.

FABRIC REQUIREMENTS

Foreground: $9^1/_2$" square of dark fabric

Flower: $4^1/_2$" square

Corners: two 4" squares, each cut once on the diagonal to make 4 triangles

Directional print: five 2" x 4" rectangles

Other supplies:

    Thread that closely matches the foreground fabric

    Dressmaker's carbon paper

    Dried-up ballpoint pen

    Basic sewing supplies

Reverse appliqué using a directional print

Assembly

Transfer the pattern onto the foreground fabric, and follow the reverse appliqué procedure of "place, baste, needle-turn, and trim" to secure the flower fabric first and then secure the corner shapes. Press gently.

Positioning a Directional Print

1. Leaving a manageable seam allowance, cut away one of the remaining pattern shapes to make a window. Place the directional fabric underneath, move it around until you are satisfied with its position, and secure it with pins. After checking to ensure that the background fabric extends beyond the marked edge of the cutout shape, baste on the outside of the line.

2. Needle-turn and trim, completing each shape before moving onto the next. Remove the basting stitches, and press the sample. To finish, reduce the seam allowance on the wrong side.

Reverse appliqué using prepared background shapes

Add interest and depth to any project by using the paper-foundation method to construct background shapes. Make them in advance, then use the patchwork shapes in the same way you would use any of the fabric pieces outlined for the previous samples.

Reverse appliqué using a prepared background

FABRIC REQUIREMENTS

Foreground: 9¹/₂" square of a light colored fabric
Background:

One 6¹/₂" square of leafy fabric for the wedges
Two 4" presewn Log Cabin squares for the corners
One 4¹/₂" diameter Crazy Log Cabin for the flower

Other supplies:

Thread that closely matches the foreground fabric
Dressmaker's carbon paper
Dried up ballpoint pen
Basic sewing supplies

Crazy Log Cabin flower and Log Cabin block

Assembly

1. Transfer the pattern onto the foreground fabric and follow the reverse appliqué procedure of "place, baste, needle-turn, and trim" to secure the leafy fabric in place.

2. Cut the Log Cabin squares on the diagonal, creating four triangles. Cut away one corner shape at a time to leave a window with a small seam allowance. "Place, baste, needle-turn, and trim" the Log Cabin triangles in place.

3. Trace the flower shape onto the center of a 4¹/₂" circle of tracing paper. Mark the circle for crazy patchwork: Working clockwise, start marking as shown in the illustrations. Keep rotating the circle, marking off slices, and numbering them consecutively until there is a small center. Mark the center with the lowest number.

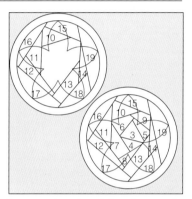

Rotate and mark until there is a small center.

4. Using a paper-foundation sewing method, work from the center to the edges, following the numbers in sequence (smallest to largest). Use a small, close stitch to perforate the paper. Add narrow fabric strips around the center until the flower shape is covered and the fabric extends to the edge of circle. Press, and remove the paper. Place and baste the block behind the marked shape before cutting away the shape and turning under the seam allowance. After appliquéing, remove the basting stitches and press the sample. To finish, trim away the excess fabric from the wrong side.

Quilting the Workshop Samples

Keep the samples on file for reference, or add borders and use them as quilt squares, pillow centers, or panels for a tote bag. The photo below shows three blocks sewn together and rounded off to make a small runner.

Place the pressed blocks, right side up, onto batting and backing, and baste or safety pin the three layers together. Quilt by sewing from the right side on the background fabric as closely as possible to the edge of the cutout shape in the foreground fabric, commonly referred to as stitching "in-the-ditch." This will encourage the quilted shapes to puff up through the cutouts in the foreground fabric.

Add outline or textural quilting on the inside of these "in-the-ditch."

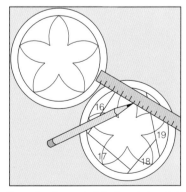

Trace the flower inside the circle, divide the circle, and number from the edge.

Reverse appliqué runner

The Projects

The projects in this section illustrate the great variety of pattern and design in metalwork. They start simply and increase in difficulty, building on the "place, baste, needle-turn, and trim" techniques you learned in the Beginner's Workshop. The final project, *The Garden Gate*, uses them all. For some projects, I have included alternative techniques for your development and students' projects to inspire construction, color, and fabric possibilities.

Patterns are included for all of the projects. Draft a "Master Pattern" by tracing same-size patterns, or by using a photocopy machine to enlarge the pattern to the desired size. Note that you need to make multiple copies of the patterns. A full-size pattern for *The Garden Gate* is in the pullout section in the back of the book.

Have a go, learn, and above all, enjoy!

PLEASE NOTE: *Fabric requirements are based on a 42" width; many fabrics shrink when washed, and widths vary by manufacturer.*

Cast-Iron Inspirations

Cast-iron production started when technical advances made it possible to melt iron into a liquid form. In contrast to wrought iron, which was very individual with no two pieces the same, cast iron was poured into pre-pared molds, allowing the mass production of identical objects. These products became easily and cheaply available for repeated forms such as railings and decorative motifs, and for designs in relief such as firebacks and grates. These days, cast iron can be seen wherever we look, and circles are a common element in these designs.

PROJECT 1

Pillows Influenced by Cast-Iron Designs

Finished size: 18" square

The lovely cast-iron design on the pillow in this project provides you with the opportunity to build on the skills you learned in the Beginner's Workshop. There are curves and points to practice, and straight lines to keep parallel. You will learn to increase the size of your square with an

Cast-Iron Pillow 1

added border that is highlighted with a strip of bright fabric to frame the design. A wrought-iron scroll is used as a quilting design on the border to make an attractive framework around the center square.

FABRIC REQUIREMENTS

Foreground fabric: 1 yard of dark blue for pattern square, border strips, and pillow back

Background fabrics:

$3/_8$ yard of floral print for square and binding

$1/_8$ yard of medium blue tone-on-tone for corner shapes

Fat quarter of bright yellow for accent and inner border

Lining (for quilting the pillow front): one 22" square

Batting: one 22" square

Cutting

TIP: *Cut the square slightly larger than necessary to allow for possible shrinkage of the foreground square that may occur during reverse appliqué.*

Foreground fabric: Cut one 14" square for the pillow center, two $3^1/_2$" x $12^1/_2$" strips for top and bottom borders, and two $3^1/_2$" x $18^1/_2$" strips for side borders. The remaining foreground fabric will be used to make the pillow back.

Floral print fabric: Cut one 11" square; cut and join sufficient 2"-wide straight strips to measure 84" for the double binding.

Medium blue: Cut four 4" squares.

Bright yellow: Cut one 7" square for pattern center; cut the remainder into four $3/_4$" x $12^1/_2$" strips for the seam inserts.

Assembly

1. Prepare a Master Pattern and transfer it, centered, onto the right side of the 14" square of foreground fabric. (See page 14 for more information.)

2. Working with one fabric square at a time, keeping in mind the straight grains of the fabric, follow the reverse appliqué procedure of "place, baste, needle-turn, and trim" (see page 24 for more information) until the design is complete. Press gently, and trim the square to measure $12^1/_2$".

3. The seam inserts add a hint of brightness to frame the center square. Fold and press each strip, with wrong sides together, along the length. Baste them, with raw edges even, around the edges of the square. They will not add to the overall size of the square.

4. Position and pin the $3^1/_2$" x $12^1/_2$" borders to the top and bottom of the square. Sew using a $1/_4$" seam to hold the inserts in the seam and to join the border strips to the square. Press away from the center square. Sew the $3^1/_2$" x $18^1/_2$" borders to the sides and press in the same way to complete the pillow top. The seam insert will now be about $1/_8$" wide.

5. Enlarge, then transfer the scroll quilting pattern, centered, onto the border strips. Place the prepared front onto the batting and lining in preparation for hand or machine quilting. Quilt from the center to the edges, stitching in-the-ditch. Also quilt $1/_4$" in from the edges to echo the shapes and emphasize the circle in the design. Trim away the excess batting and lining to an $18^1/_2$" square.

6. Prepare the pillow back to measure $18^1/_2$" square with an overlap or zipper (see page 16 for more information). Pin the pillow front onto the pillow back, with raw edges even and wrong sides together. Bind the pillow to complete (see page 19 for more information).

Now that you've made one pillow, here are three similar cast-iron patterns so you can make a matching set for that favorite spot in your home.

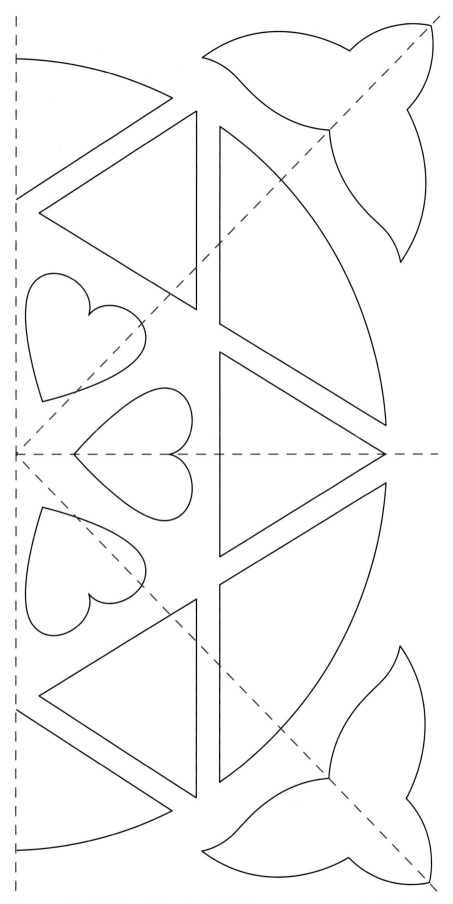

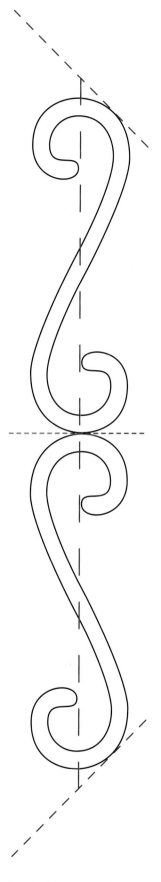

Pattern for *Cast-iron Pillow 1*. Enlarge by 121%. Make two copies to create the Master Pattern.

Scroll quilting pattern for the pillow border. Enlarge by 257%.

Cast-iron Pillow 2

Pattern for *Cast-iron Pillow 2*. Enlarge by 129%. Make four copies to create the Master Pattern.

Cast-iron Pillow 3

Pattern for *Cast-iron Pillow 3*. Enlarge by 129%. Make four copies to create the Master Pattern.

Cast-iron Pillow 4

Pattern for *Cast-iron Pillow 4*. Enlarge by 128%. Make four copies to create the Master Pattern.

Pillow (pattern 4), Loretta Bailey, Bretton, Cheshire, England

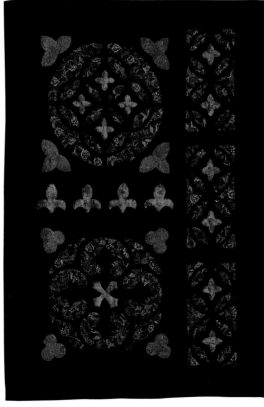

Water Lilies (patterns 2 & 3), Denise Willis, Heald Green, Cheshire, England

Pillow (pattern 3), Julie Scoffield, Prestatyn, Denbighshire, Wales

Wallhangings Using Repeat Patterns from Grilles and Grids

Repeat patterns lend themselves to a variety of uses. Consider them for gate designs and border patterns, drafting them to the length and width you need for your wallhanging. You will need to make multiple copies of the patterns to create the Master Pattern. The wallhangings featured in Projects 2 through 5 show some of the different styles that can result when using the "place, baste, needle-turn, and trim" method and a little imagination. Don't forget that small wallhangings make welcome gifts for the special somebody who appreciates the love that is sewn into them!

These projects build on the Beginner's Workshop, providing further opportunity to practice the skills learned. New ideas are presented in each project, such as quilting the background fabric before the appliqué, or constructing the background in a more dynamic way. It's time to grow a little!

PROJECT 2

Through the Grille Wallhanging

Finished size: 18" x 22"
Reverse appliqué using one background fabric

This wallhanging was my contribution to The Suitcase Collection of the Quilters' Guild of the British Isles. Each region in the guild invited members to make a small wallhanging that would fit into a standard suitcase without folding. Each of these easily portable collections could be exchanged between regions to allow wider exposure of the quilts through mini-exhibitions.

The background is a single batik fabric chosen to suggest a watercolor painting. Free-motion machine quilting of natural designs and textures, such as flowers, leaves, sky, and water, complements the background.

Through the Grille. A broken frame $1/2$" wide was added to the Master Pattern.

TIP: *If you are a machine quilter, it is easier to quilt the background fabric first, before placing it behind the foreground fabric. Use a low-loft batting to keep the work flat, and baste the marked foreground fabric well before needle-turning the edges of the shapes.*

FABRIC REQUIREMENTS

Foreground fabric: 1 1/8 yards black (includes backing, binding, and hanging sleeve)

Background fabric: fat quarter of a colorful batik

Batting: 22" x 26"

Cutting

Foreground fabric: Cut one 19" x 23" rectangle for the foreground, one 22" x 26" rectangle for the backing, and a 4" x 17" strip for the hanging sleeve.

Cut and join sufficient 2"-wide straight strips to measure 90" long for the double binding.

Assembly

1. Prepare a Master Pattern on graph paper, and transfer it, centered, onto the foreground fabric.

Pattern for *Through the Grille* Wallhanging. Enlarge by 114%. Make multiple copies to create the Master Pattern.

(See page 14 for more information.)

2. Center and baste the batik onto the batting and backing in preparation for machine quilting. Have fun with your machine by drawing with the needle to produce natural forms or textures. (See page 18 for more information.) Relax, play, and enjoy!

TIP: *If you prefer to hand quilt, complete the reverse appliqué first, then stitch-in-the-ditch to enhance the pattern shapes.*

3. Center the marked foreground fabric over the quilted background fabric. Baste between the pattern shapes to hold the layers together.

4. Cut out, clip, needle-turn, and sew the shapes using a matching thread and concealed stitches. Stitch only into the batik fabric; avoid taking stitches through all the layers.

5. Trim the outer edges to 18" x 22". Prepare and add a hanging sleeve along the top back edge. To complete the wallhanging, bind the edges. (See page 18 for more information.)

Rainbow Grid Wallhanging

Finished size: 9" x 24"
Reverse appliqué using a directional print

I only had a long quarter yard (9" x 42") of this colorful directional fabric and had to use it economically to get the bias-cut binding out of it as well as the background. After completing the reverse appliqué, I machine quilted the piece at $1/4$" intervals to emphasize the run of color through the fabric. You may wish to add embellishments such as tassels or buttons.

FABRIC REQUIREMENTS

Foreground fabric: $3/4$ yard dark fabric (includes backing and hanging sleeve)

Background fabric: long quarter yard (9" x 42") directional rainbow print

Batting: 13" x 28"

Rainbow Grid

Cutting

Foreground fabric: Cut one 9" x 24" strip for the foreground, one 13" x 28" rectangle for the backing, and one 4" x 8" strip for the hanging sleeve.

Background fabric: Cut one 9" x 22" strip. From the remainder, cut and join sufficient $1^{1}/4$" bias strips to make a 71"-long single binding.

Assembly

1. Prepare a Master Pattern (9" x 24") and transfer it, centered, onto the foreground fabric. (See page 14 for more information.)

2. Leaving a $1/4$" seam allowance, cut out a complete shape at the top and the bottom of the marked foreground fabric. Place the directional print behind the foreground, and use the cutouts to check the placement of the print before basting the layers together. Cut out, clip, needle-turn, and sew each of the shapes. (See page 24 for more information.) Trim from the back to remove excess fabric.

3. Lay the top on the batting and backing, and baste for machine or hand quilting. Quilt vertical lines at $1/4$" intervals on the background shapes to emphasize the lines of color.

4. Trim away the excess fabric and shape the lower edge to a 45° angle. Prepare and add a hanging sleeve, and bind the edges to complete. (See pages 18-19 for more information.)

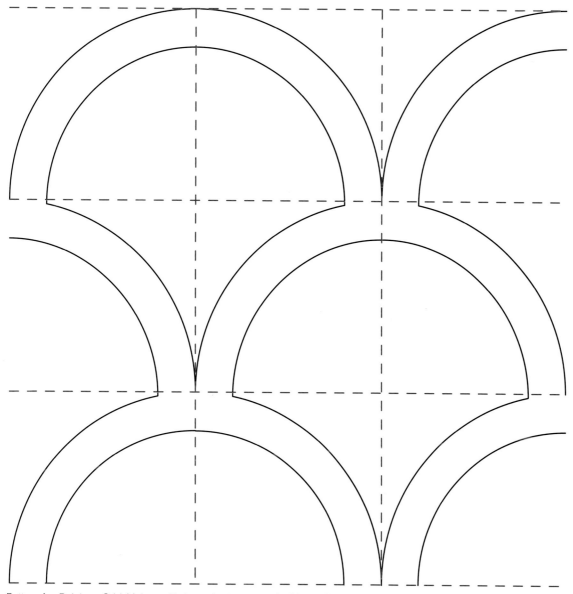

Pattern for *Rainbow Grid*. Make multiple copies to create the Master Pattern.

Christmas Bellpull

Finished size: 10" x 42"
Reverse appliqué using two background fabrics

Influenced by the old-fashioned bellpull, this wall decoration is the easiest of hangings to use in the home. Because it is long and thin, it can be an eye-catching feature beside a fireplace or bookcase, or in an alcove or hall. In Christmas fabrics it can be a table runner beneath a seasonal center-piece. The design uses two background fabrics. It is machine quilted with an allover grid that ignores the pattern shapes.

FABRIC REQUIREMENTS

Foreground fabric: 1 yard dark green fabric (includes backing and binding)

Background fabrics: long quarter yard (9" x 42") of both a medium Christmas floral and a contrasting solid red

Batting: 14" x 46"

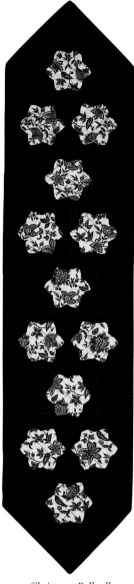

Christmas Bellpull

Cutting

Foreground fabric: Using the full width of the dark fabric (from selvage to selvage), cut a 10" strip for the foreground and a 14" strip for the backing. Cut and join sufficient 2" straight strips to measure 122" long for the double binding. (See page 18 for more information.)

Assembly

1. Prepare a Master Pattern and transfer it, centered, onto the foreground fabric. (See page 14 for more information.)

2. Place the strip of floral fabric behind the foreground fabric. Baste only around the pattern shapes where this fabric will appear. Cut out, clip, and needle-turn the shapes using a matching thread and a concealed stitch. Trim from the back to remove excess fabric. (See page 22 for more information.) Press gently.

TIP: *An uncut strip of background fabric placed behind the foreground, although a bit wasteful, helps stabilize your work and makes sewing easier.*

---

3. Place the contrasting fabric in a strip behind the foreground fabric; baste, clip, needle-turn, and trim.

4. Mark a 2" grid, placing the ruler at 45° to the vertical sides to set the squares on point. Place the foreground onto the batting and backing, and quilt by machine. (See page 18 for more information.)

5. Trim and shape the outer edges and bind to complete. (See page 19 for more information.) Sew a ring onto the back for hanging.

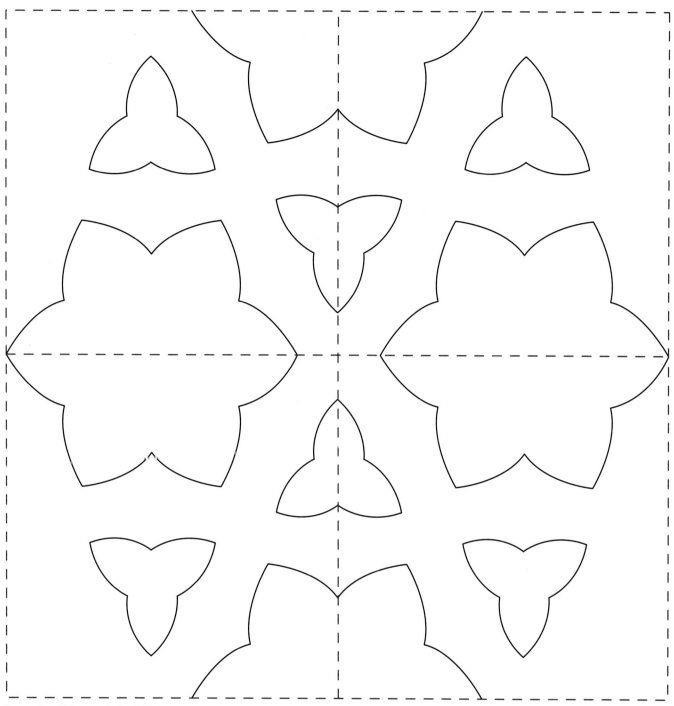

Pattern for *Christmas Bellpull*. Enlarge by 111%. Make multiple copies to create the Master Pattern.

Autumn Crosses Wallhanging

Finished size: 10" x 27"
Reverse appliqué using several background fabrics

This small wallhanging shows the effectiveness of combining scraps of fabric with a strong foreground fabric. The autumnal tones of the foreground fabric help to unite the scraps, and the shading of the scraps from yellow to orange to red adds good visual impact. It is made using the "place, baste, needle-turn, and trim" method.

FABRIC REQUIREMENTS

Foreground fabric: $7/8$ yard dark fabric (includes backing and binding)
Background fabric: 4" squares of bright scraps that shade from yellow through orange into red
Batting: 14" x 31"

Cutting

Foreground fabric: Cut a 10" x 27" foreground strip and a 14" x 31" backing strip. Cut and join sufficient 2" straight strips to make a double binding 78" long for the edge. (See page 18 for more information.)

Assembly

Working one square of background fabric at a time, use the "place, baste, needle-turn, and trim" method to complete this project following the steps outlined in Project 4.

Autumn Crosses

Dyeing to Paint Wallhanging

Finished size: 38" x 41"
Reverse appliqué using a prepared background fabric

Jo Ann, a quilting friend from Georgia, dyes her own fabric in graded colors. She has given me some samples over the years. It's lovely just to enjoy these palettes of color, to fondle the fabrics, and to reflect on how clever she is. But there comes a time when you have to decide that the fabrics aren't too good to use, and you need a project that will show them off to their full advantage. This vibrant project, influenced by a wallhanging by Melody Johnson, was planned as an exercise in the movement of color using dyed fabrics.

The pieced background fabric consists of random-width strips sewn diagonally onto square paper foundations. These squares

Dyeing to Paint

Pattern for *Autumn Crosses*. Enlarge by 111%. Make multiple copies to create the Master Pattern.

were cut into quarters and sewn into rows. The basic square measures $6\frac{1}{2}$" because that just happens to be the size of my square ruler. When quartered, this results in $3\frac{1}{4}$" "building blocks." I staggered the rows of squares to eliminate bulky seams and provide a gentle transition from one color to the next.

The background of *Hydrangea Fence* (page 84) was constructed using this method.

Before adding the foreground fabric for reverse appliqué, the background was machine quilted with free-motion designs.

FABRIC REQUIREMENTS

Foreground fabric: $1\frac{3}{8}$ yards dark purple fabric (includes the borders and binding)

Background fabric: 3 yards graded, dyed fabrics of your chosen color palette

Backing: $1\frac{1}{2}$ yards (includes hanging sleeve)

Batting: 42" x 45"

Cutting

Cut forty-six $6\frac{1}{2}$" paper foundation squares.

Dyed fabrics: Cut all of the dyed fabrics into strips of varying widths from 1" to $2\frac{1}{2}$" wide. You could start by cutting a few strips from each fabric and cut more as needed.

Backing: Cut a rectangle 42" x 45", and an 8" x 37" strip for a double hanging sleeve.

Foreground fabric: Cut a 39" x 42" rectangle. Cut and join sufficient 2" straight strips to make a 168"-long double binding.

Assembly

Prepare the background fabric as follows:

1. Using a small, close stitch, sew the strips onto the paper foundation squares until the paper is covered. Press. Aim for a gentle transition through the graded colors and from one color into another. Vary the direction of the strips from square to square to add interest.

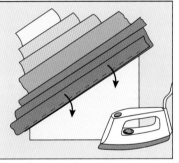

Cover the paper foundation squares with fabric strips and press.

2. Trim away the excess fabric to the edge of the paper. Remove the paper by tearing along the perforated lines left by the small stitches. Cut each large square into four smaller squares to create the basic building blocks.

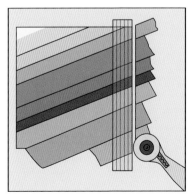

Trim off the excess fabric.

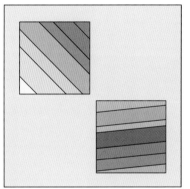

Cut the square into four $3\frac{1}{4}$" squares for the "building blocks."

3. My quilt contains 182 small squares (cut from 46 larger ones). Prepare many of these building blocks before attempting to play with them on a design wall.

"Paint" with the squares by staggering and rotating them to add interest; the strips should move in all directions. Arrange the squares, turn them, and arrange them again until you are pleased with the result. You may want to make some individual $3\frac{1}{4}$" squares if there are specific gaps to fill.

Pattern for *Dyeing to Paint*. Enlarge by 110%. Make multiple copies to create the Master Pattern.

The background fabric in the sample contains 13 squares across and 14 squares down; it measures 36¼" x 39".

4. Trim away any excess fabric to straighten the edges. Baste the pieced background fabric, centered, onto the batting and the backing, allowing about 3" of batting and backing all around. Machine quilt.

TIP: *When learning to machine quilt, be prepared to devote a few projects to "practice" before you become comfortable with the method. Use this as a learning project, knowing that it is going to be overlaid with a foreground grid. Use threads to* match the various colors so the stitches blend into the background. Just enjoy drawing with the needle, creating different patterns and textures.

5. Measure the quilted background fabric, and draw a rectangle on graph paper equal to that exact size. Inside the rectangle draw another line ³/₄" all the way around to allow for a comfort zone. Prepare a Master Pattern to fit within the comfort zone. (See page 14 for more information.)

6. Transfer the pattern, centered, onto the foreground fabric. (See page 21 for more information.)

TIP: *For a visually pleasing result, be aware of the vertical and horizontal pattern lines, and line them up with the vertical and horizontal seams of the pieced background.*

7. Cut out, clip, and needle-turn to appliqué the shapes using matching thread and concealed stitches.

8. Trim the outer borders to measure 38" x 41", squaring the edges. Prepare and add a double hanging sleeve, and bind to complete. (See page 18 for more information.)

Gallery of Student Quilts

Lesley's Grid (pattern 2, using several fabrics), Lesley Kendall, Northwich, Cheshire, England

Mary's Grid (pattern 3, using a prepared background), Mary Williams, Bomere Heath, Shropshire, England

Flowers in the Window (pattern 3, using a prepared background), Loretta Bailey, Bretton, Cheshire, England

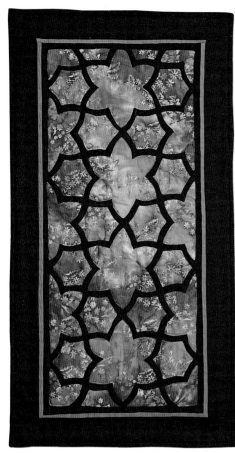

Arabian Window (using one background), designed by Dot Aellen, Heald Green, Cheshire, England

Barbara's Bellpull (pattern 6, using a prepared background of foundation-pieced chevron), Barbara Lane, Warrington, Cheshire, England

Turkish Delight (using a prepared background of a colorwashed chevron designed by Dilys), Liz Pedley, Drury, Flintshire, England

Carol's Grid (pattern 6, using one background fabric), Carol Clee, Prestatyn, Denbighshire, England

Jan's Colorwash Grid (using a prepared background in colorwash and a grid designed by Dilys), Jan Huxley, Hoole, Cheshire, England

From the East Window of Carlisle Cathedral (using one background), designed by Jane Hadfield, Cheadle Hulme, Cheshire, England

Leaded Window Designs

As well as providing a view and letting in light, windows are a source of pattern and inspiration. The simple grids in many leaded windows are as appealing to me as those in metal gates. When looking through a window to see the scene beyond, the eye takes in the design of the window itself, just as it sees the gate when you look through it into a garden.

Producing glass in large sheets was impossible until fairly recently, so leaded grids were used to separate and support the small individual panes of plain glass. From simple, repeated geometric settings these grids developed into a variety of imaginative designs. Grids were also used in the construction of fanlights, the semicircular inserts above doors that allow light to filter into otherwise dark hallways, and they could be simply or ornately decorative.

More complex design in leaded windows is apparent in the magnificent circular windows known as "rose windows," which are a feature of some of our early churches and cathedrals. Suspended between heaven and earth like mandalas, they contrasted dramatically with the stone and shadow of early cathedrals, inviting the onlooker to be one with God. Initially they were architecturally convenient and involved cooperation between the clergy, stonemason, blacksmith, and glazier. However, they soon became associated with symbolism as the wheel of life, the radiating star, and the light of the world.

Each section in a rose window consists of small panes in a repeated geometrical setting, but it is the stonework that gives the overall design and character to this window. In Victorian times, circular windows were built into churches to let more light into the buildings.

PROJECT 7

Christmas Rose Tree Skirt

Finished size: 42" in diameter. A tree skirt inspired by rose windows

This circular quilt is a Christmas tree skirt, but it can also be made as a stunning table centerpiece. You may prefer to make it in colors to match your decor so you can use it all year long.

FABRIC REQUIREMENTS

Foreground fabric: 1¼ yards Christmas red

Background fabrics: ½ yard of each of the following:
    Christmas white for the center motif and round 3
    Green with gold for round 1
    Christmas floral for round 2
    Green with red for round 4

Border fabric (optional): 1¼ yards for the optional prairie-points border, or ¼ yard for a plain bias binding

Backing fabric: 46" square

Batting: 46" square

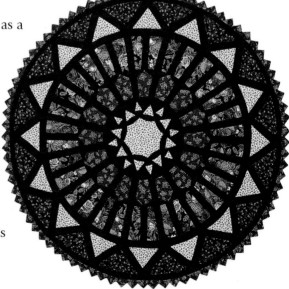

Christmas Rose

Cutting

Background fabrics:

Christmas white: Cut one 12" square for the center. Cut four 7" squares, then cut twice diagonally to make 16 quarter-square triangles for round 3.

Green with gold: Cut sixteen 3½" x 5" strips for round 1.

Christmas floral: Cut thirty-two 3" x 6½" strips for round 2.

Green with red: Cut four 9" squares, then cut twice diagonally to make 16 quarter-square triangles for round 4.

Assembly

1. Make the Master Pattern of the complete circular design, including the outer cutting edge by enlarging the pattern on a photocopy machine. (See page 14 for more information.)

2. Transfer the pattern, centered, onto the right side of the foreground fabric using dressmaker's carbon paper. (See page 21 for more information.)

3. Place each prepared background fabric shape behind the appropriate foreground marked shape. Baste, needle-turn, and trim until the design is complete. (See page 24 for more information.)

4. Gently press the finished top. Baste it onto the batting and backing layers, and quilt. Trim all the layers to the outer marked pattern line, making a 42" circle.

5. From the fabric chosen to make the prairie points, cut seven 6"-wide strips from selvage to selvage. Using diagonal seams, join the strips into a continuous length. Make the continuous prairie points. (See page 16 for more information.) With the points lying inward, pin the prairie points to the top layer only of the tree skirt, matching the long fold to the raw edge. Attach them to the edge of the skirt using a ¼" seam. Maneuver the first and last points to interweave them, and complete the circle. From the front, press the points so they extend outward. Working from the back, turn under ¼" on the edge of the backing fabric, and sew this down by hand over the back of the prairie points to cover the seam.

Harvest Rose, designed by Dilys, made by Kath Lloyd, Drury, Flintshire, Wales, 2001

Julie's Rose, designed by Dilys, made by Julie Scoffield, Prestatyn, Denbighshire, Wales, 2001

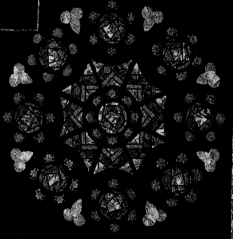

Hoffman Rose, Dilys Fronks, 2000

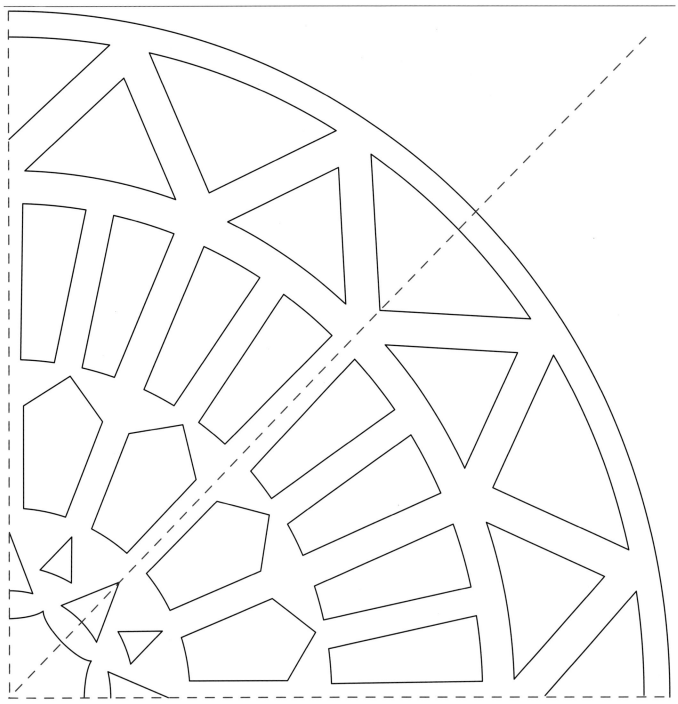

Pattern for *Christmas Rose*. Enlarge by 278%. Make multiple copies to create the Master Pattern.

Leaded Lights

I am often asked to teach in church halls. It was while teaching reverse appliqué influenced by metalwork in such a hall in Dunoon, Scotland, that I noticed the leaded window panels in the doors. I pointed them out to the students as a source of inspiration and to illustrate that we were surrounded by design ideas if we took time to actually look. A student photographed them and sent the pictures to me after the workshop. I automatically set about interpreting one in reverse appliqué.

This type of metal grid is a uniform width throughout, so I am often asked whether it would be better to use continuous bias strips instead of my traditional method. One of the advantages of my reverse appliqué method is that it eliminates the need to prepare vast lengths of bias tape. However, since the introduction of ready-made iron-on bias tape, you can use the bias tape to interpret leaded lights, as shown in the projects that follow.

Examples of leaded window designs from *A Booke of Svndry Dravghtes (leaded glafs)*, 1615, reproduced in facsimile in 1898 by The Leadenhall Press Ltd., London.

Leaded-Glass Garden Wallhanging

Finished Size: 24" x 28"

This project features a leaded window design with a view beyond. Although the step-by-step instructions are for a wallhanging the size of the sample, it is worth noting that the grid can easily be drafted to any size using a ruler and compass on graph paper, or enlarged on a photocopy machine. The background picture must measure 2" larger on each side than the grid pattern to allow for a comfort zone.

FABRIC REQUIREMENTS

Background fabrics: eight different fabrics for the background picture. Select fabrics that suggest a gentle flow of color across the background.

> Fabrics 1-4, 6-8: $\frac{1}{8}$ yard each
>
> Fabric 5: $\frac{1}{4}$ yard

Black fabric: $\frac{1}{3}$ yard for inner border and binding

Tone-on-tone fabric: $\frac{1}{3}$ yard for border fabric (walls)

Wood-grain fabric: $\frac{1}{8}$ yard for border fabric (window sill)

Black iron-on bias tape: 15 yards

Backing fabric: 1 yard (includes hanging sleeve)

Batting: 28" x 32"

Leaded-Glass Garden

Cutting

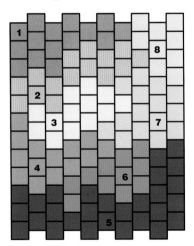

Patchwork grid for the picture

Background fabric: Cut each fabric into $2\frac{1}{2}$" squares.

> Fabric 1, 2, and 7: Cut 15 squares.
>
> Fabric 3: Cut 13 squares.
>
> Fabric 4: Cut 14 squares.

Fabric 5: Cut 28 squares.

Fabric 6: Cut 11 squares.

Fabric 8: Cut 9 squares.

TIP: *Instead of piecing the background, you may consider using a suitable preprinted picture panel or a color-washed picture, and draft the grid to fit.*

Inner border strips: Cut two 1" x $21\frac{1}{2}$" strips and two 1" x 25" strips.

Outer border: For the sill, cut one strip 3" x 25", and for the walls, cut one strip 3" x 25" and two strips 3" x 29". These dimensions allow for mitered corners.

Backing and hanging sleeve: Cut one 28" x 32" rectangle for the backing, and one rectangle 4" x 23" for the hanging sleeve.

Binding: Cut and join sufficient 2" straight strips to measure 114" for the double binding.

Assembly

1. Referring to the photo and the assembly diagram, compose the background with the $2\frac{1}{2}$" background squares on your design wall. Refer to the construction method used in the *Garden Gate* project. (See page 74 for more information.)

2. On graph paper, make a Master Pattern (page 14) of the complete grid using the 6" wide x 4" high section. The pattern for the sample measures 18" x 22".

3. Clearly transfer the pattern as a single line onto the center of the right side of the prepared picture.

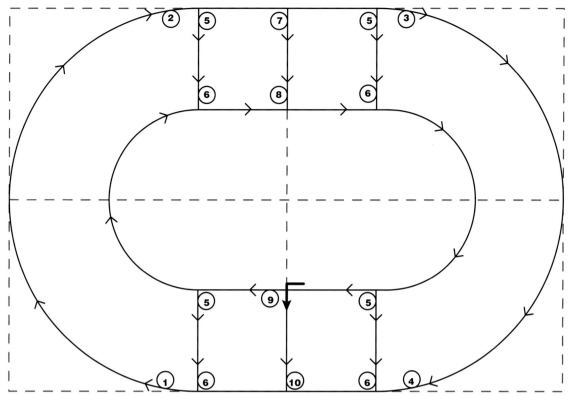

Pattern for *Leaded-Glass Garden.* Make multiple copies to complete the Master Pattern.

Be aware of the vertical and horizontal pattern lines, and line them up with the vertical and horizontal seams of the pieced background.

TIP: *The lines need to be visible. If this proves difficult with dressmaker's carbon, try the following method: Trace the pattern onto good quality tissue paper, and pin it onto the right side of the picture. (See page 17 for more information.) Machine sew along the lines, using a contrasting thread and small stitches that perforate but do not tear the paper as you sew. Remove the paper, leaving the stitched pattern lines.*

4. Following the manufacturer's instructions, peel the paper backing off the bias tape a little at a time, and center the tape on top of the marked pattern line. Iron it onto the background, making sure that right angles are sharp and curves are smooth. If you follow the suggested appliqué sequence, the raw ends of the bias strips will

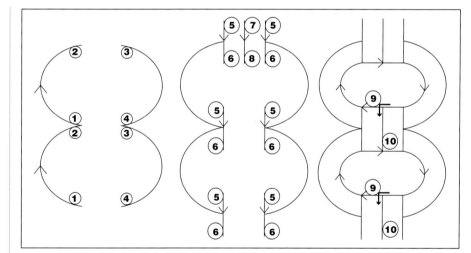

Add bias following these diagrams.

be covered by other bias strips. When complete, the ends of the bias tape should extend $1/2$" beyond the edge of the background. Sew the bias in place by hand, using matching thread and concealed stitches.

TIP: *If you prefer to machine appliqué the bias strips, baste the picture onto the batting and backing. Sew both edges of the*

bias tape using a blind hemstitch and monofilament thread. Or use a matching thread and straight stitches. Either method will appliqué and quilt the hanging in one step.

5. Press gently on the wrong side, and trim the excess background fabric around the edge, leaving a $3/16$" seam allowance beyond the marked pattern line.

Flowers in the Window (Master pattern not given.)

6. Add the inner border strips first and then the outer border strips, mitering the corners. (See page 15 for more information.)

TIP: *If you are machine appliquéing, add the borders by sewing through the batting and backing.*

---

7. Place the bordered picture onto batting and backing fabric in preparation for quilting. Baste, then quilt by hand or machine, stitching in-the-ditch as close as possible to the bias tape. If you are competent with free-motion machine quilting, consider adding some textural lines to the background picture. Add any preferred quilting lines to the border. Trim the outer edges of the picture, prepare and add a single hanging sleeve, and bind to complete. (See page 18 for more information.)

Leaded Stained-Glass Wallhanging

Finished size: 14" x 26"

This wallhanging uses a leaded window design as a stained-glass pattern. To create a repeat pattern for use behind the grid, use my quick, template-free method: Mark the pattern on the wrong side of the light foundation fabric, and appliqué the background fabrics in sequence onto the right side.

FABRIC REQUIREMENTS

Foundation fabric: 14" x 26" white fabric (this will be visible in the completed design)

Background fabrics: $3/8$ yard each of a medium-scale floral for the rings, a purple for the straight grid, and a yellow tone-on-tone for the diagonal grid

Black: $1/3$ yard for border and binding

Black iron-on bias tape: 18 yards

Backing fabric: $1/2$ yard (includes hanging sleeve)

Batting: 18" x 30"

Leaded Stained Glass

Cutting

Background fabrics: Cut into manageable squares and strips that are about $3/4$" larger all around than the appliqué shapes needed.

Black fabric: Cut two $1\frac{1}{2}$" x $12\frac{1}{2}$" strips and two $1\frac{1}{2}$" x $26\frac{1}{2}$" strips for the border. Cut and join 2" straight strips to measure 90" for the double binding.

Backing fabric: Cut one 18" x 30" rectangle for the backing and one 4" x 13" strip for the hanging sleeve.

Assembly

1. On graph paper, make a Master Pattern (page 14) of the complete grid using the 6" x 6" section. The pattern for the project measures 12" x 24".

2. Trace the pattern as a single line onto the wrong side of the foundation fabric. This marked side will be the wrong side of the work, and all the sewing will be done along the marked lines on this side. The unmarked side is the right side; place all fabrics right side up on the unmarked side. The sample steps that follow illustrate the sequence.

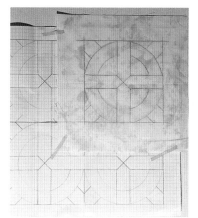
Trace the pattern onto the wrong side of the foundation fabric.

3. Work with one appliqué shape at a time, positioning it right side up on the unmarked side of the foundation fabric to cover the shape where it will appear. Check its position by holding it up to the light to see where it will show on the grid; pin it in place. Make sure the grain lines match those of the foundation fabric.

Pin the appliqué shapes right side up on the right side of the foundation.

4. Using contrasting thread and small hand or machine stitches, sew the shape in place, sewing along the marked line on the wrong side. Sew all around the shape.

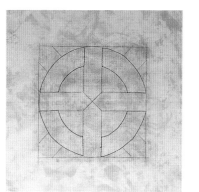
On the wrong side, sew on the line around each shape to secure it in place.

5. On the front, cut away any excess fabric, leaving a scant $1/16$" seam allowance on the outside edge of the stitches.

Trim the fabric on the right side.

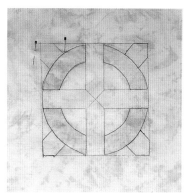
Position another appliqué shape right side up, and secure by sewing on the wrong side.

Trim the fabric on the right side.

6. Repeat the sequence of "position, pin, sew, and trim" for all the fabrics to complete the design.

TIP: *Be aware that you will sew along the same line twice when you are securing adjacent shapes.*

Apply the iron-on bias tape.

The completed pattern

Leaded Stained Glass (detail)

7. Following the suggested sequence, and referring to the photo of the quilt for placement, iron the bias tape, centered, on top of the sewing lines. Each line of

the pattern will start with an odd number and finish with an even number, to show where you will start with the bias tape and where you will stop.

Sew in place by hand or machine.

8. Add the outer borders (see page 15 for more information), place onto batting and backing, and quilt. Trim the outer edges.

9. Prepare and add a single hanging sleeve. (See page 18 for more information.) Bind to complete.

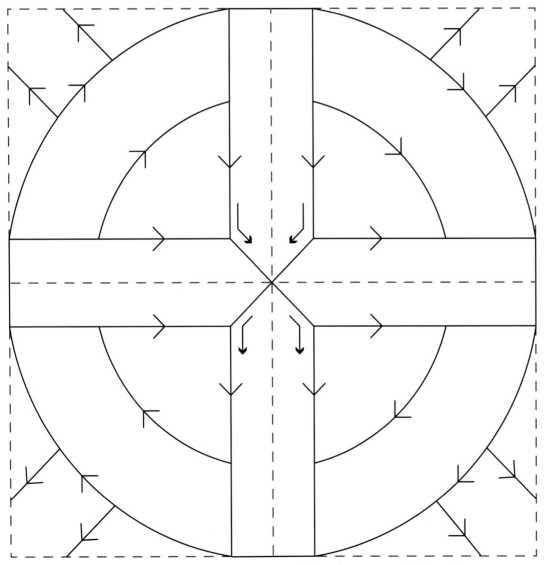

Pattern for *Leaded Stained Glass*. Enlarge by 104%. Make multiple copies to create the Master Pattern.

Follow the numbers and arrows until you understand the sequence and path for ironing on the bias tape. If you follow this diagram carefully, the only unfinished or uncovered ends will be around the outside edge. Enlarge 130% for easier readability.

Fanlights

Fanlights provide another source of inspiration for designs. They are everywhere in the United Kingdom, and there is plenty of variety. You can look through the glass and framework to witness the changing skies beyond. At night the focus changes to the fanlight's patterns themselves, which are best appreciated from the outside with the light shining through from inside.

Fanlight no. 60

London Fanlight

Fanlight no. 92

Fanlight no. 17

Twice, with limited success, I have tried to make a quilt in the gate series entirely by machine that stands up to my own standards for display and scrutiny. I have mastered the machine-quilted background, but I still prefer to appliqué the gate by hand.

To machine appliqué successfully, I feel there should be fusible web behind the foreground fabric to hold the fabric layers together and stop the edges from fraying for the length of time the piece of work is handled. I have tried this successfully on smaller pieces that are easily maneuverable through the machine, but I foresee only problems when trying to use fusible web on a large gate pattern. The foreground fabric, with its cutout pattern, would be unwieldy and extremely unstable until it was pressed onto the picture. And even if I could bond the pattern successfully, I would still face the problem of machine stitching a large quilt. A quilt made up of intricate metal patterns that twist, turn, and rotate as they do in the gate designs would be especially difficult to machine appliqué with a satin stitch.

Fanlight no. 80

Photos by Dilys Fronks

If you are a skilled machine sewer, you may wish to try using fusible webbing for a small project. The fanlight pillow designs are manageable on the sewing machine, and are quilted at the same time they are appliquéd. If you prefer, you can appliqué by hand, following the "place, baste, needle-turn, and trim" method.

Pillows Influenced by Fanlight Designs

Finished size: 18" square

One pattern is used for this pillow, but three other patterns are included to create a matching set for a family room or bedroom.

FABRIC REQUIREMENTS

Foreground fabric: ⅞ yard navy (includes pillow back and binding)

Background fabric: fat quarter of batik

Fusible web: one 16" square

Backing fabric: one 22" square

Batting: one 22" square

Fanlight Pillow 1, Sylvia Wood, Swinton, Lancashire, England, 2001

Cutting

Foreground fabric: Cut one 19" square. Cut and join sufficient straight strips to measure 84" for a double binding.

Background fabric: Cut one 16" square.

Assembly

1. Make a Master Pattern of the design (see page 14 for more information).

2. Trace the fanlight design accurately onto the paper side of the fusible web. Trim away the excess fusible around the outer edges of the fan shape, leaving ½" beyond the edge of the pattern.

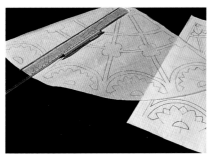

Trace the pattern onto fusible web.

3. On the ironing board, lay the fusible web, with the traced pattern shape centered, on the wrong side of the foreground fabric square, paper side up. Press, following the manufacturer's instructions. Let it cool.

Iron the fusible web onto the wrong side of the foreground fabric.

4. Using small, sharp scissors, carefully cut out the shapes to be discarded, leaving the pattern of the fanlight. Do not remove the paper until you are ready to sew.

Cut out the pattern shapes using sharp scissors.

TIP: *Trim the smaller shapes first. (If the paper lifts, the pattern will be displaced.)*

5. Place the background square, right side up, on the ironing board. Carefully remove the paper backing from behind the foreground grid, and place the foreground fabric on top of the background fabric, making sure that it lies flat.

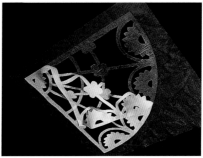

Remove the paper backing from behind the grid.

6. Starting in one corner, carefully press the grid in place, being aware that you only have one attempt to get it right! Cut away the excess background fabric that lies outside the edge of the fused pattern.

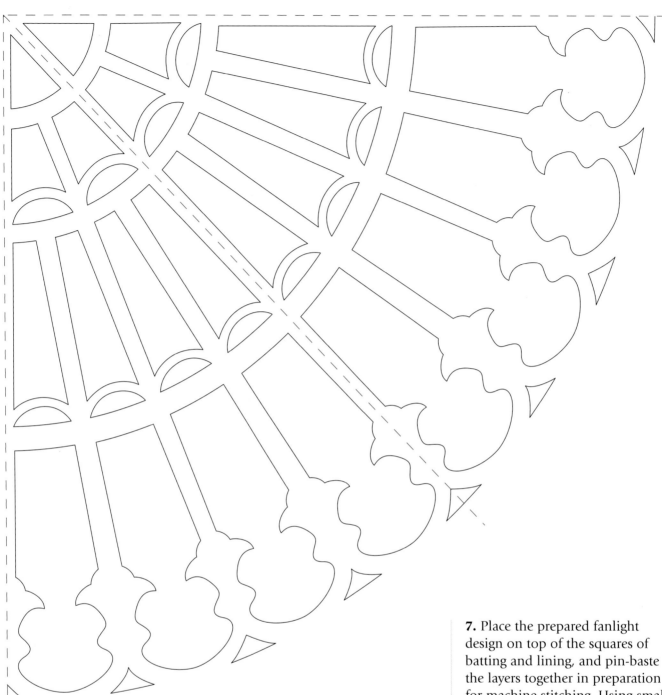

Pattern for *Fanlight Pillow 1*. Enlarge by 214%.

Press the cut-out grid onto the right side of the background fabric.

7. Place the prepared fanlight design on top of the squares of batting and lining, and pin-baste the layers together in preparation for machine stitching. Using small, controlled zigzag stitches and matching thread, sew along the fused edges of the design, machine appliquéing and quilting at the same time. Add any other quilting lines or textures.

8. Trim the squares to $18^{1}/_{2}$". Prepare a pillow back with an overlap or a zipper and bind. (See pages 16 and 18 for more information.)

Fanlight Pillow 2, Liz Pedley, Drury, Flintshire, Wales, 2001

Pattern for *Fanlight Pillow 2*. Enlarge by 444%.

Fanlight Pillow 3, Liz Pedley, Drury, Flintshire, Wales, 2001

Pattern for *Fanlight Pillow 3*. Enlarge by 453%.

Fanlight Pillow 4, Sylvia Wood, Swinton, Lancashire, England, 2001

Pattern for *Fanlight Pillow 4*. Enlarge by 453%.

Fanlight with a Patchwork Sky

Finished size: 32" x 19"

As an extension of Project 10, here are two of the fanlight designs used as they were originally intended—as windows with sky visible beyond. The background skies, which must be prepared in advance, are made up differently—one in patchwork, the other in appliqué. This fanlight project is machine appliquéd using the method explained with Project 10.

Summer Fanlight

FABRIC REQUIREMENTS

Foreground fabric: ³/₄ yard textured (includes binding)

Background fabrics: ¹/₄ yard each of fabrics 1-4 for the patchwork picture (including two sky, one foliage, and one floral fabric)

Backing fabric: 1 yard (includes hanging sleeve)

Fusible web: 1 yard

Batting: 36" x 23"

Samples of fabric used in Summer Fanlight

Cutting

Foreground fabric: Cut a rectangle to measure 33" x 20". Cut and join sufficient 2" straight strips to measure 112" for a double binding.

Background fabrics: Cut each fabric into 2¹/₂" squares as follows:

    Fabric 1: Cut 27 squares.

    Fabric 2: Cut 39 squares.

    Fabric 3: Cut 25 squares.

    Fabric 4: Cut 22 squares.

Backing fabric: Cut one 36" x 23" rectangle for backing; cut a 4" x 31" strip for hanging sleeve.

Assembly

1. Prepare the Master Pattern (see page 14 for more information) for the fanlight of your choice from the patterns on pages 56-57, making it a semicircle.

2. Following the method detailed in Project 10, page 55, trace the pattern accurately onto the fusible web. Trim away the excess, leaving ¹/₂" beyond the edge of the drawn pattern.

3. Using the photo and assembly diagram for reference, compose the background with the 2¹/₂" squares on your design wall. Refer to the construction method used in *The Garden Gate* project. (See page 73 for more information.)

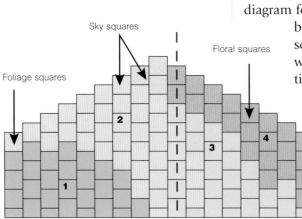

Sky squares

Floral squares

Foliage squares

Patchwork grid for
Summer Fanlight

4. Press, then trim the lower edges even.

5. Center, then press the fusible webbing onto the wrong side of the foreground fabric. Cut out the pattern. (See page 55 for more information.)

6. Place the background picture right side up on the ironing board. Remove the paper backing from the pattern. Carefully position the pattern on top of the picture, making sure that, where appropriate, the vertical or horizontal lines of the pattern run parallel to the seams of the background picture. Carefully press the foreground pattern so it adheres to the picture. From the back, cut away the excess background fabric that lies beyond the edge of the fused pattern.

7. Place the fused fabric onto the batting and backing, and baste them together. Machine appliqué the fused edges of the design, using matching thread and small zigzag stitches. Add any other desired outline or textural quilting lines.

8. Trim the outer edges of the picture to measure 32" x 19". Prepare and add a single hanging sleeve. (See page 18 for more information.)

9. Bind the edges to complete the design. (See page 18 for more information.)

PROJECT 12

Fanlight with an Appliqué Sky

Finished size: 32" x 18"

In this fanlight project, the picture is quilted before it is layered with the foreground pattern. There is textural machine quilting on the picture, but I needle-turned the edges of the marked fanlight pattern by hand. I now use this procedure regularly to make my gate quilts, and it is successful because I sew with the fabrics flat, using a tabletop method (page 14).

FABRIC REQUIREMENTS

Foreground fabric: ³⁄₄ yard black fabric (includes binding)

Background fabric: Scraps of tone-on-tone fabrics that suggest a sunrise, from the palest yellows through oranges to the deepest reds

Foundation fabric: 33" x 17" rectangle of lightweight fabric for the appliqué sky

Backing fabric: ³⁄₄ yard for backing and hanging sleeve

Batting: 36" x 22"

Sunrise Fanlight

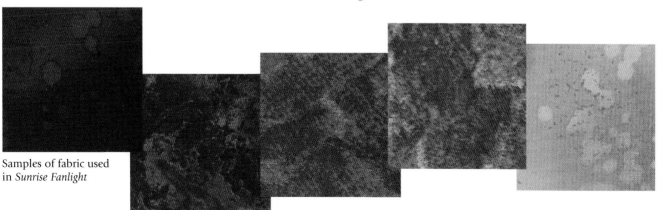

Samples of fabric used in *Sunrise Fanlight*

Cutting

Foreground fabric: Cut one 33" x 19" rectangle. Cut and join sufficient 2" straight strips to measure 110" for a double binding.

Backing: Cut one 36" x 22" rectangle for backing; cut a 4" x 31" strip for hanging sleeve.

Assembly

1. Prepare the Master Pattern of your chosen fanlight, making it a semicircle. (See page 14 for more information.) Use a ruler to extend the pattern lines and open out the corners, as seen in the sample. The pattern will measure 30" x 15".

2. On graph paper, draw a 32" x 16" rectangle, and divide it into 4" sections. Draw in the sky pattern, referring to the diagram Use the pattern shapes to make freezer-paper templates. The freezer-paper templates are ironed shiny side down with a dry iron, onto the right side of the fabric. Remember to add the seam allowance to each shape. Appliqué the sky shapes onto the foundation fabric using your preferred method of sewing, by hand or machine.

3. Place the finished picture onto the batting and backing, and baste the layers together in preparation for machine quilting.

4. Quilt using lightweight, matching cotton threads. Draw the rays of the rising sun, define cloud-like textures, outline some clouds, and draw undulating shapes and gentle atmospheric lines. (See page 18 for more information.)

5. Using dressmaker's carbon paper, transfer the pattern, centered, onto the right side of the foreground fabric. Follow the "place, baste, needle-turn, and trim" method to sew the fanlight to the picture. (See page 24 for more information.)

6. Straighten and trim the outer edges to measure 32" x 18" using a rotary cutter and a large ruler. Prepare and add a single hanging sleeve. (See page 18 for more information.)

7. Bind to complete the quilt. (See page 18 for more information.)

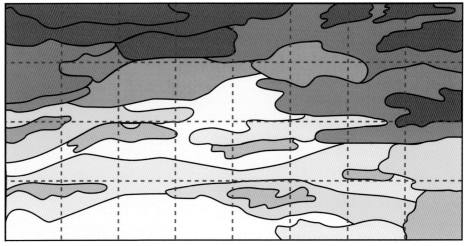

Pattern for the appliqué sky

Quilts Inspired by Wrought-Iron Designs

There are three basic features used in the construction of wrought-iron gates and fences: the S scroll, the C scroll, and a decorative spike. Once the metal bars have outlined the linear structure, these simple shapes provide the decorative elements. Patterns for these shapes and a simple heart are featured with the following project, so you can make templates to try your own designs. They can be used in many combinations to create different designs, as seen in the lap quilt.

The lap quilt features six such designs. Although quite different, all the designs have been placed in the same circular setting, which unifies the finished blocks. The repetition of the placement of the different fabrics, from the center to the edge of each block, also helps to unite the designs into a pleasing quilt. To permit the most economical use of the fabric, the quilt blocks are rectangles instead of the usual squares.

Simple wrought-iron pattern shapes

Lap Quilt Using Simple Wrought-Iron Motifs

Finished size: 51" x 65"
Finished block size: 20" x 18"
Finished inner border: $1\frac{1}{2}$"; finished outer border: 4"

FABRIC REQUIREMENTS

Foreground fabric: $3\frac{1}{2}$ yards dark teal fabric (includes outer border and binding)

Background fabrics:

Light floral: $1\frac{3}{4}$ yards for circular border and inner quilt border

Medium teal tone-on-tone: $\frac{3}{4}$ yard for wrought-iron motifs

Light teal tone-on-tone: $\frac{7}{8}$ yard for inner circle

Medium mauve tone-on-tone: $\frac{1}{4}$ yard for center motifs and $\frac{1}{2}$ yard for optional prairie points

Backing fabric: 55" x 69" ($3\frac{1}{4}$ yards)

Batting: 55" x 69"

Wrought-Iron Lap Quilt, blocks made by Jean Anderson, Mary Greenwood, Lesley Kendall, Barbara Lane, Pip Sumbler, and Denise Willis, designed by Dilys, 2001

Cutting

Foreground fabric: Cut six 20" x 22" rectangular blocks along the lengthwise grain (parallel to the selvage).

Cut sixteen 1" x 2" strips and four 2" squares for inner border.

Cut two $4\frac{1}{2}$" x $43\frac{1}{2}$" strips for the top and bottom outer borders.

Cut two $4\frac{1}{2}$" x $65\frac{1}{2}$" strips for the side outer borders.

Cut and join sufficient 2" straight strips to measure $6\frac{1}{2}$ yards for a double binding.

Floral for inner border: Cut four 2" x 10" strips and four 2" x $10\frac{1}{4}$" strips for the top and bottom inner border.

Cut eight 2" x 9" strips and four 2" x $9\frac{1}{4}$" strips for the side inner borders.

Assembly

1. Prepare a Master Pattern of the six designs and transfer each one, centered, onto the right side of the foreground rectangles. (See pages 14 and 21 for more information.)

2. Prepare the blocks using the reverse appliqué method of "place, baste, needle-turn, and trim." (See page 24 for more information.) Work with one fabric at a time, and be aware of the straight grains of the fabrics. (See page 11 for more information.) Cut manageable squares and rectangles from the floral, light, medium, and contrasting fabrics.

3. Referring to the assembly diagram, trim all the blocks to $18\frac{1}{2}$" x $20\frac{1}{2}$", and join them together in sequence.

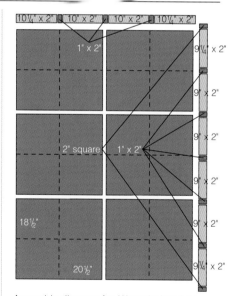

Assembly diagram for *Wrought-Iron Lap Quilt*. Measurements are cut sizes.

4. Join the inner border strips together in sequence, then sew them to the blocks using a $\frac{1}{4}$" seam allowance.

5. Add the outer border strips to the inner border to finish the quilt top.

6. Position the quilt top onto the batting and backing, and baste. Quilt by hand or machine. The sample was marked with cross-hatched lines at 2" intervals. It was quilted by machine using matching thread and a decorative stitch.

7. To make the optional prairie points, cut two 8" x 44" strips from the contrasting fabric. Use these to prepare the prairie points, following the illustrated method shown on page 16. Separate them into four rows of ten points each, and pin them onto opposite corners of the quilt, as shown in the sample.

8. Bind to complete. (See page 18 for more information.)

Block 1. Enlarge by 125%. Make two and two mirror images to create the Master Pattern.

Block 2. Enlarge by 125%. Make two and two mirror images to create the Master Pattern.

Block 3. Enlarge by 125%. Make four copies to create the Master Pattern.

Block 4. Enlarge by 125%. Make four copies to create
the Master Pattern.

Block 5. Enlarge by 125%. Make four copies to create the Master Pattern.

Block 6. Enlarge by 125%. Make four copies to create the Master Pattern.

The Garden Gate Wallhanging Project

As my interest in wrought iron as a decorative design source developed and my collection of gate and fence patterns grew, I experimented with different ways of using them. At first, I used selected metal patterns as designs for quilt blocks, adding the background fabrics in a balanced, regular way to emphasize the metalwork shapes. These blocks, used in isolation, resulted in the quilts *Overwrought I* and *II* (page 7). Later, I realized that the effect of the patterns wasn't lost when you looked through them. In fact, the detail beyond the metal grids often accentuated and complemented the patterns.

About this time in the quilt world there was a growing trend to use fabrics for colorwashed and watercolor effects, with books detailing the technique. My first thoroughly enjoyable attempt at a geometric pattern in colorwash reawakened in me an abiding love for jigsaw puzzles, and this encouraged me to develop the idea further. So, by combining a watercolor garden "painted" with fabric squares and a wrought-iron design, I conceived the gate quilts. The original concept behind these quilts was to represent what you would see when looking from under a shaded tree toward the light in the distance. Anything in front of the light, such as a gate, grasses, or leaves, would be silhouetted, and so followed the decision to appliqué the foreground in black.

There are two distinct stages to the step-by-step method in the garden gate project. The first stage is "painting" the garden using fabric squares. Then a gate and border are added as the foreground to add extra interest and give a feeling of perspective.

The explanation of the method that follows is divided into two parts. The first part offers advice on a free approach to the method, to encourage originality in picture-making and creativity in designing your own gate. The other part is devoted to the construction of a watercolor picture, created with specific fabrics to a set grid, to fit the pullout pattern at the end of the book.

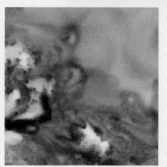

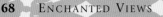

Spring Gate, 31" x 32". This is the quilt made using the pullout pattern for the gate. Photo by Peter West

Fabric samples for the *Spring Gate* quilt

Basic Steps for a Garden Gate Project

1. Choosing a scene: Choose a picture that has good composition and is easily interpreted.

2. Selecting the fabrics: Choose fabrics that help interpret what you wish to show.

3. Preparing a design wall: Make a vertical design wall so you can build the scene and view it from a distance.

4. Preparing the fabric squares: Cut your fabrics into 2½" squares.

5. Testing the fabric potential: Familiarize yourself with the fabrics by testing them on your design wall.

6. Painting the scene: Position the squares to create the picture, staggering the rows.

7. Reviewing the scene: Appraise the scene before sewing the pieces together.

8. Sewing the squares together: Check and label the squares, then sew into rows.

9. Squaring the edges: Trim the excess fabric from the top and bottom of the picture.

10. Drafting the wrought-iron design pattern: Measure the picture and draft the gate pattern to size.

11. Transferring the design: Transfer the pattern using dressmaker's carbon paper.

12. Overlaying the design: Position the pattern on top of the picture and baste the layers together.

13. Needle-turning the edges: Cut away each shape and sew the edge onto the background.

14. Assembling and quilting the quilt: Use the quilting process to create loft, texture, and detail.

15. Completing the quilt: Prepare a hanging sleeve, bind the edges, and label.

FABRIC REQUIREMENTS FOR QUILTS MADE WITH THE PULLOUT PATTERN

Foreground fabric: 1 yard black

Background fabrics for picture: ¼ yard each of eleven fabrics

Backing fabric: 1 yard (a 35" x 36" piece for the backing, and a 4" x 30" strip for the hanging sleeve)

Batting: 35" x 36"

CHOOSING A SCENE

For inspiration for your scene, use photographs, gardening books, magazines, greeting cards, sketches, and so on. Because squares are the most convenient building blocks for making the picture, plan to interpret your composition loosely to give a general impression rather than a stone-by-stone, leaf-by-leaf representation. Choose a picture with good composition, one that is easily broken down into features that simplify the look of the scene. This will make the picture easier to use and still allow for flexibility in design. Take your inspiration from the pictures and quilts featured in this section (pages 70-77).

You may have already learned the principles of colorwash from another teacher's workshop or created a watercolor quilt using one of the many books on the subject. Perhaps you can use one of these methods, or you might prefer the simplicity of using a preprinted panel or enjoy the challenge of creating a complex scene that calls for intricate appliqué or painstaking piecing. The choice is yours.

Mair's Garden, 22" x 32", Mair Scott, Wrexham, Flintshire, Wales, 2001

Shades of Autumn background. This picture was made using different fabrics but the same grid as *Spring Gate*, and it will work with the pullout pattern.

Fabric samples for the *Shades of Autumn* quilt

When referring to my own work, I usually like to distinguish between colorwashing and watercoloring with fabric. A colorwash method uses many different fabrics to interpret a geometric pattern. It emphasizes smooth transition from light to dark by using the values of the fabric. In contrast, to paint a watercolor garden, I use fabrics in a limited palette to interpret what I see: leafy fabrics for

trees and hedgerows, florals for flower borders, textures for water and sky, stony fabrics for pathways, and so on.

I prefer to work without a picture, to let the design flow by using the fabrics in my stash and seeing where they lead me. I habitually place the darker fabrics at the bottom and outer edges of the design and the lighter values at the top and center of the scene.

If you are working to the set grid (page 73), the features have been identified already and the scene suggested.

SELECTING THE FABRICS

Once you have decided whether your source of inspiration will be picture-based or fabric-based, pull your fabrics together to make a loose interpretation of the scene, aiming for gentle transitions from one fabric to the next. Fabric selection will be easier if you can divide the composition into features, such as a pathway, a water element, a bower of flowers, a bank of trees, and so on.

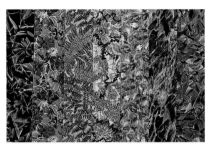

Samples of undergrowth fabrics

Samples of path fabrics

Samples of foliage fabrics

Samples of fabrics showing grasses

Samples of flower fabrics

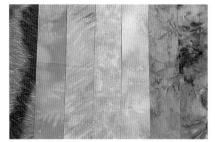

Samples of sky fabrics

Samples of water fabrics

Look for the following ranges of fabrics, the busier the better:

- Earthy fabrics for ground and undergrowth
- Grassy and stony fabrics for borders, walls, and pathways
- Leafy fabrics: light, medium, and medium-dark shades; large and small leaves
- Floral fabrics: large, medium, and small prints on both light and dark backgrounds
- Sky fabrics: nothing solid in appearance but interesting blues, greens, yellows, and pinks
- Water fabrics: green-blue fabrics that suggest movement

Get into the habit of checking the reverse side of each fabric for a softer effect, to give a feeling of depth, and help make the transition toward lighter tones.

If you are working to the set grid (page 73), the fabrics used for *Spring Gate* are shown on pages 68 and 69. A second garden, following the same grid but with another palette of fabrics, results in a totally different look. (See *Shades of Autumn* on page 71.) Try choosing from your own fabric stash to personalize your grid.

THE DESIGN WALL

A design wall is essential for creating a scene. You can make one simply by stapling a flannel sheet or piece of batting to the wall. Or you can use a portable design wall, made by stapling flannel onto a rigid board. Place it at a comfortable height for good visual appraisal as you work. Prepare as generous a space as possible to give yourself room for exploring the potential of the fabrics and encouraging freedom in the flow of the watercolor picture.

The fabric on the wall needs to be taut enough to hold the fabric squares indefinitely. Then you can work confidently, without fear of them dropping off overnight or when your back is turned. To encourage free, spontaneous positioning and repositioning of the squares, there should be no need for pinning. It really is a chore if you have to pin your squares, move them, and pin them again. I find that this can discourage the flow of creativity. Keep in mind that $1/2$" will be lost from each square in the construction process.

To fit the pullout pattern for the garden grid, a working area of 40" x 45" will allow for 16 rows of 17 squares each.

PREPARING THE FABRIC SQUARES

From the feature fabrics, be prepared to cut at least two $2\frac{1}{2}$"-wide strips from selvage to selvage to yield enough squares to work with. These are the fabrics that you are going to use to interpret the main features in your picture, such as water, a pathway, a floral arch, a hedgerow, and so on. It is wasteful to cut isolated flowers from a fabric, and it is easier to explore the potential of the fabric if you use all the colors, textures, and characteristics of the fabric.

❖ Fold the fabric to fit onto the cutting board, and iron it to hold the layers together. Straighten up the raw edges using a ruler and rotary cutter, and cut at least two $2\frac{1}{2}$"-wide strips. Without moving the strips, rotate the board and cut the strips into $2\frac{1}{2}$" squares.

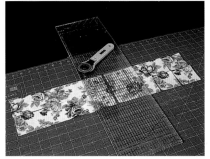

Cut $2\frac{1}{2}$" strips, rotate the board, and cut $2\frac{1}{2}$" squares.

Store the squares in small plastic food trays until you are ready to start.

The storage system

If you are working to the set grid shown below, cut the number of squares needed for each fabric as follows:

Fabric 1	42 squares
Fabric 2	19 squares
Fabric 3	4 squares
Fabric 4	27 squares
Fabric 5	16 squares
Fabric 6	14 squares
Fabric 7	12 squares
Fabric 8	32 squares
Fabric 9	25 squares
Fabric 10	42 squares
Fabric 11	39 squares

TESTING THE FABRICS' POTENTIAL

As you start to paint with your fabric squares, compare the process to assembling a jigsaw puzzle. I start a puzzle by sorting out the edge pieces first because these are the easiest to identify. When joined together, they provide a frame in which to work, thus defining the size. The size of the garden is determined by a specified grid or the size of the design wall.

The next pieces to sort are those that are easy to pick out by color or markings. Before positioning them in the completed picture, work these as mini-puzzles within the frame. In other words, test the feature fabrics (individual patterns, colors, and textures) while you can separate them and easily explore ideas with them.

It's important that you familiarize yourself with your fabrics before you attempt to compose a complete picture. Be prepared to move pieces freely at this early stage. As you play, you will start to get some idea of how you can use the fabrics or where you can place them.

Unless you need to create a strong horizon, construction is easier if you assemble the rows vertically rather than horizontally, and stagger or offset the squares from row to row. Place the squares systematically onto the design wall, edge to edge, without overlapping, so they will be easy to reposition when the time comes. Start with a strong feature, such as a multicolored floral fabric. Sort the squares into different areas of pattern, such as the dominant flowers, the leafy areas, the other significant flowers based on type or color, the background areas, and so on. Look at the wrong side of each fabric to see whether it is usable.

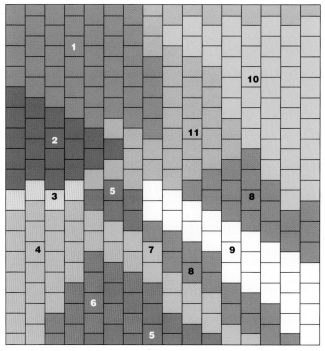

Grid for *Spring Gate* on page 69 and *Shades of Autumn* on page 71.

❖ Using a large floral fabric, place the dominant flowers on the design wall, remembering to stagger the squares vertically. Don't worry about placement, just become familiar with the fabric by handling and looking at it. Do the flowers hang, or do they stand out? Are they the same size, to create a splash of color in the foreground? Can you arrange the flowers to gently flow horizontally or vertically? Once you have arranged the major blossoms, look at other significant flowers, and fit these into the sequence so they flow from the dominant blooms. Because you have cut them from the same fabric, they will look as though they belong together. If they are smaller than the major flowers, should you place them near the front of the picture or farther away to create distance? If they are lighter, perhaps you should place them higher up, toward the sky. If they are darker, perhaps they belong lower down, toward the undergrowth. Use any leafy areas or undefined squares from the same fabric to fill in around the main spread of the flowers.

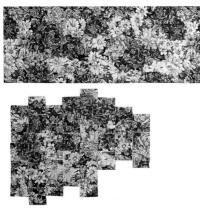

Test a floral; rearrange the blooms to unite the main spread of flowers.

In another area of the design wall, play with fabrics for another feature, such as water, to become familiar with them and judge their potential. Try a pathway; work out how to get it moving across the garden, becoming smaller in the distance.

If you are working to the set grid, familiarize yourself with the palette of fabrics in the same way, so that you know how to use the fabrics to their full potential.

PAINTING THE SCENE

Remembering to stagger the fabric squares in vertical lines, decide where to place the feature fabrics that you have explored. Move the pathway, the stream, the hedgerow, or that luscious border of flowers to establish its position so the surrounding features can be integrated and related to it. Then, establish the position of the mini-puzzles within the frame. Once they are in place, develop the rest of the picture by filling in the blanks with the elements that are not so easily defined.

The filler fabrics link the main features, creating a gentle transition between the different features. Because the aim is to avoid strong edges that stop the eye from flowing freely around the scene, you will need to choose filler fabrics of similar colors and values when moving to lighter or darker areas. Try reversing the feature fabrics to soften an edge. Or, choose busy textures to lead from one color into another: from the green of a hedge to the blue of a sky, for example, or from the brightness of a flower border to the darkness of the undergrowth.

For the best visual appraisal, work for short periods on the picture. Get into the habit of leaving it alone for a short while before coming back to get another impression. Another way of assessing your progress is to view it from a distance: Stand with your back to the design wall, as far away as possible,

and look at it through a mirror held above your shoulder. Look at the over-all scene rather than concentrating on individual squares. Or, create the same sense of distance by looking at the design through a reducing glass or the wrong end of a pair of binoculars.

If you are working to the set grid, follow the suggested placement of the various fabrics squares used in the palette.

Building up *Shades of Autumn*

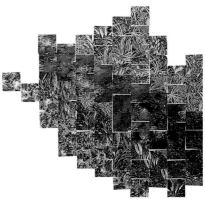

Defining the grassy border

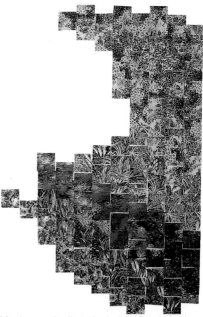

Moving vertically to include a floral shrub

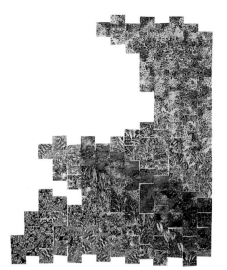

Bringing brightness to the foreground

Adding more brightness and depth

Framing with foliage and filling in the sky

Developing the color into the border

Building up *Dilys's Garden—I Wish!*

This quilt was made the same size as *Spring Gate* and *Shades of Autumn* but without the restrictions of a grid. The sequence of steps here and on page 78 is offered to help you create a quilt similar in size to *Spring Gate* using a more free-flowing approach.

Fabric samples used in *Dilys's Garden—I Wish!*

Dilys's Garden—I Wish!, 32" x 33", 2000

Gallery of Gardens

Barbara's Garden, 36" x 36", Barbara Thomas, Buckley, Flintshire, Wales, 2001

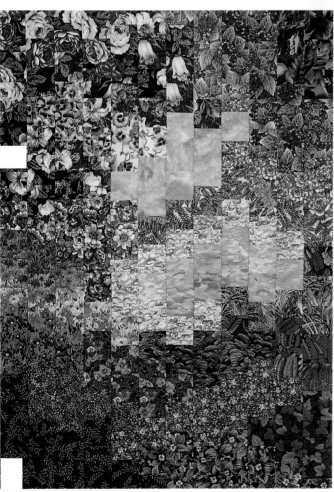

Carol's Garden, 24" x 34", Carol Clee, Prestatyn, Denbighshire, Wales, 2001

Poll's Garden, 28" x 33", Mary Williams, Bomere Heath,
Shropshire, England, 2001

Lakeside Walk, 40" x 50", Dilys Fronks, 2001

Positioning a luscious floral to create sideways movement

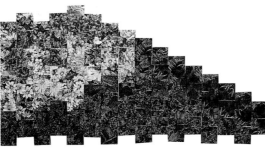

Adding a walkway, defined by a small bright border

Emphasizing the border with lighter flowers, used to create perspective

Defining the edge with darker leafy tones

Lightening the borders to create a focal point

Framing with hanging flowers to define the top edge

REVIEWING THE SCENE

There comes a time when you have to say "That's it, I'm happy with it!" Leave it overnight if possible, and view it fresh in the morning.

❖ Check that the squares in each row offset those in the adjoining rows. Check also that the ends of the rows stagger up and down, in sequence, at both the top and bottom. Make adjustments as necessary.

❖ Count the number of squares in each row. There may be the same number, or there may be one extra in alternate rows.

❖ Label the first squares in each row, from left to right, in alphabetical order. Indicate with an arrow whether the row starts in an up or down (offset) position.

If you are working to the set grid, you will have 17 squares in each row, with row A marked as a "down" row, B as an "up" row, and so on.

SEWING THE SQUARES TOGETHER

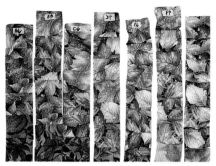

Label the rows, pin the seams, and sew the squares together into rows.

❖ The squares need to be pinned together first to ready them for the machine. With raw edges together, pin them accurately for a $\frac{1}{4}$" seam, so that there is no need to stop and readjust them before chain piecing them together. Pin from right to left, so the point of the pin will go toward the sewing machine during chain piecing. This will make the pins easier to remove during sewing.

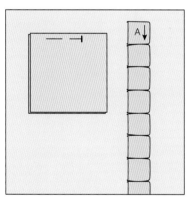

Pin the squares into rows.

❖ After pinning the squares into vertical rows, pin them back, in sequence, onto the design wall. If you don't own enough pins to do all the rows, pin a few, and sew them so you can reuse the pins.

I developed a chain-piecing method that uses thread economically: I sew one row at a time. When I tried to alternate between two rows, they became twisted and the pins fell out, causing confusion.

❖ Sew the seam between squares 1 and 2, removing the pin as the needle approaches.

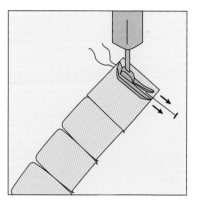

Sew the seam and remove the pin.

Skip the next three pins in the row, and position the fourth seam beneath the sewing foot, with the point of the pin toward the needle.

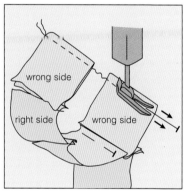

Skip every three pins, and sew the fourth.

Feed the fabrics through the machine so that you can remove the pin easily once you have started the seam.

When you get to the end of the row, sew across a folded scrap of fabric, making a bridge. This will release the row, so you can cut the threads between the squares. Start again, sewing the seam between squares 2 and 3, and repeating the process until you have sewn the whole row.

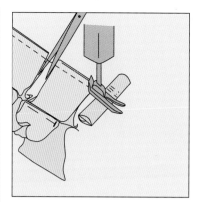

Use a bridge to release the row, and trim the thread.

❖ Press all the seams from top to bottom, and pin the row back onto the design wall. Continue until you have sewn all the rows and returned them to the design wall. Double check to be sure that the strips lie in sequence and that you have not made any obvious errors in stitching the rows or arranging them on the wall.

To join the rows, finger-press to find the centers of several squares at regular intervals down the lengths of all the alternate rows: A, C, E, G, and so on. Lay row A on a flat surface, right side up, and, with right sides together, place row B on top. Being aware of the stagger, line up the appropriate seams of row B with the creases in row A. Pin the seams to the creases along the length of the row, and feed them through the sewing machine. Remove the pins only when they are almost under the needle to prevent slippage.

❖ Working in sequence, pin the sewn pairs back on the design wall, and repeat the procedure to join all the rows to complete the picture. From the back, press all the seams in the same direction. From the front, check to make sure there are no tucks in the seams.

Pin and sew the rows, staggering the seams.

If you are working with the set grid, join square to square to make the rows, and row to row to the complete the picture in the same way.

SQUARING THE EDGES

❖ Cut away the staggered pieces at the top and bottom of each row to straighten the edges: Lay the picture, right side up, flat on a cutting board. Place a ruler along the uneven edge to be trimmed. Line up the vertical lines on the ruler so they are parallel with the vertical seams, ensuring that you cut the edges at right angles to the seams. Trim with a rotary cutter, and repeat for the other staggered edge.

Trim the staggered edges.

❖ Measure the pieced background fabric, and make a note of the ver-

tical and horizontal measurements through the middle of the picture.

If you are working with the set grid, even the edge in the same way. If you have sewn the seams accurately, the picture should measure $32\frac{1}{2}$" x $33\frac{1}{4}$". To allow for inaccuracies in construction, the picture should measure no less than 31" to fit the pullout pattern.

DRAFTING THE WROUGHT-IRON PATTERN

❖ Tape large sheets of graph paper together, and draw a rectangle to match the vertical and horizontal measurements of your background picture. Mark the centerlines. Draw a $\frac{3}{4}$" border all around the inside of the marked rectangle to establish a comfort zone. This inner line is the edge of the pattern and the start of the black border. There must be no part of the silhouette (gate, grasses, leaves, and so on) beyond this line. Design your gate and leafy border within this area.

The following information will be helpful if you would like to design your own gate.

• The gate can be square or rectangular, and it should come about three-quarters of the way up the space.

• It can be a double gate, a single gate, or just a decorative fence.

• The gate needs to hang at least 1" above the ground. Join it to a portion of fence or to the border.

• A gate hangs on hinges, but a fence needs to be fixed into the ground for support.

• The most common gate designs can be divided into vertical and horizontal sections. Fill them

with the common S and C scrolls in a variety of combinations.

• The gate's structural bars should be $\frac{1}{4}$" wide, except allow $\frac{1}{2}$" around the edge of the gate or fence. Increase these widths to $\frac{1}{2}$" and 1" for a large picture.

• Add interest to the edge with silhouetted leaves, twigs, foliage, and grasses.

• You can adapt any of the patterns and designs in the other projects to fit your prepared picture, as shown in the sequence that follows.

• The aim is to draft a pattern in which everything is connected to form a network of holes that you can cut from the black fabric.

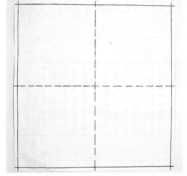

Prepare the graph paper to the size of the picture. Add the vertical and horizontal centerlines and a $\frac{3}{4}$" comfort zone all the way around.

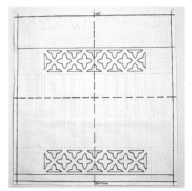

Define the gate by leaving a 1" gap under the gate, and draw a line across the top of the gate. Add a decorative panel, centered, to the top and bottom of the gate.

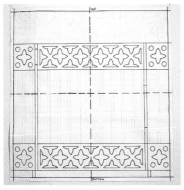

Add hinges and a fastener, leaving a ½" gap before starting the fence. Use the pattern motif to fill in the space.

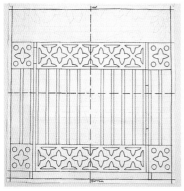

Add matching vertical supports to each side of the center.

Fill any large spaces, and decorate the top of the gate with pattern elements such as scrolls. Add leaf shapes to soften the border.

Use a black marker to define the holes.

The pattern, ready for use

If you have been following the set grid, the pullout gate pattern will fit your picture. Make a Master Pattern by tracing the two sections.

TRANSFERRING THE PATTERN

The black foreground fabric needs to be a good quality, lightweight cotton to reduce the chances of fraying. It needs to be larger than the silhouette pattern because the border is an integral part of the pattern. You will know the size of the design area—within the marked comfort zone. To this dimension, add the size of your preferred black border, between 1" and 3" all the way around.

❖ Cut the black fabric to size. Finger-press to find the vertical and horizontal centers, and baste along these lines with a contrasting thread. Press to remove the creases and secure the fabric, right side up, on a flat surface with masking tape.

TIP: *Press the black fabric at this stage. With some brands of carbon paper, the markings disappear under the heat of the iron, which makes later pressing inadvisable!*

❖ Matching the centerlines of the pullout gate pattern with those of the fabric, position the pattern on top of the fabric. Pin or tape the pattern securely along only one long edge of the fabric, outside the lines of the pattern. For best results, use yellow or white dressmaker's carbon paper. Read the manufacturer's instructions before testing it to make sure that it will transfer a good, clear line onto your foreground fabric.

❖ Carefully lift the pattern sheet, and slide the carbon, colored side down, between the pattern and the fabric. Pin the pattern down around all the edges now. Avoid putting pins into the carbon paper because you may need to move it.

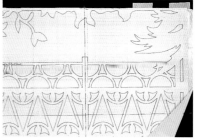

Center the pullout pattern on top of the black fabric, and slide the carbon paper between the layers.

❖ Use a ballpoint pen to transfer the pattern lines onto the fabric. You can hold it comfortably, applying sustained pressure over a long period, and the metal tip will transfer the line well. If you want to avoid marking your pattern, use a dried-up pen. Use a ruler for straight lines. Transfer a small portion of the design and check the quality of the line before continuing. Take time to transfer the pattern clearly and accurately onto the fabric.

Work methodically, and get into the habit of thinking of the cutout design elements as holes. Draw around a complete hole, and mark the center with a pencil. That way, if you are disturbed in the middle of the transferring process, you will know where you have been and where you need to go.

OVERLAYING THE GARDEN DESIGN

The rows of squares are joined together with vertical seams, so it follows that the vertical lines of the gate or fence pattern must parallel these seams. (If you have joined your squares in horizontal rows, match the seams with the horizontal pattern lines.)

❖ Fold the picture to find the center points on all sides, which will be either a seam or the center of a square. Mark each center with a pin, positioning the head toward the outer edge for easy removal. Tape the picture (background), right side up, on a flat surface.

❖ Fold the black fabric in half vertically, right sides together, so that the basted line runs along the fold.

❖Place the black fabric on top of the picture so that the folded edge runs right down the middle of the picture, from pin to pin, to match the centers. Also check to see that the horizontal basting runs from pin to pin.

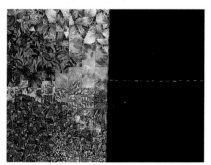

Position the vertical centerfold down the middle of the picture, and line up the horizontal center with the horizontal basting line.

❖ Carefully open out the black fabric so it lies flat, without shifting it from its centered position. Remove the pins from the picture underneath, and reposition them on top to hold the gate to the picture. Place additional pins into the marked line around the edge of the foreground pattern. Lift the black fabric to confirm that the picture extends at least $3/4$" beyond the pins marking the edge of the pattern; this extension is your comfort zone. Make certain that the vertical seams run parallel to the vertical pattern lines by feeling the seam and drawing in-the-ditch with a fingernail. These impressions must parallel the marked pattern lines. If they do not, readjust the black fabric until they do, for the best visual results.

❖ To secure the layers, pin well all over. Baste the layers together by sewing down the middle of the wrought-iron pattern lines. Baste $1/4$" away from the straight border and leafy edges. This is the last time you will see the complete picture until you have turned all the edges of the pattern. It should be sufficient encouragement to get the reverse appliqué done!

Baste $1/4$" away from the marked line.

NEEDLE-TURNING THE EDGES

The edges of the marked pattern need to be cut and needle-turned in order to expose the picture underneath. There is no rule about working from the center out to the edges. As long as the layers are

basted together well, there should be no movement of one against the other.

Cut away the fabric, leaving $3/16$" on the inside of the marked line.

❖ Cut and needle-turn one hole in the foreground fabric at a time, eventually leaving the gate superimposed on the background picture. Follow the needle-turning method detailed in the Beginner's Workshop. (See page 22 for more information.) Once the sewing is complete, cut away any areas of the picture remaining behind the leaves and outer borders of the foreground fabric. Leave $1/4$" seams.

❖ Decide on the width of the borders. Use a rotary cutter and ruler to square up the corners, and trim away the excess fabric to even the raw edges.

ASSEMBLING AND QUILTING THE QUILT

My first gate, *Cheltenham Gate* (page 86), was extensively hand quilted with different textures, but you have to examine it closely to see that it is handwork. On my next gate, *Gothic Gate* (page 1), I machine quilted, with mediocre results. So I practiced on other quilted items until I became more competent and confident. I started quilting my large *Open Gate* (page 4) quilt by hand in the more visible sky areas as I plucked up the courage to try by machine. A deadline approached, and I had little choice in the end but to machine quilt it. I tried lots of textures, often using ones suggested by the fabrics themselves or by their function in the picture. Now I machine quilt all of my gate quilts.

❖ Press the completed picture carefully from the back. Cut the batting and backing to measure a minimum of 2"than the black fabric larger all the way around.

❖ Baste the three layers together in preparation for quilting by hand or machine. The minimum amount of quilting that you need to do is to quilt in-the-ditch on both sides of the wrought iron and around the silhouetted features. For added interest, quilt veins on the silhou-etted leaves, scrolls on the black border, and textural lines. (See page 18 for more information.)

COMPLETING THE QUILT

❖ Trim the excess fabric, and square off the corners. Prepare a hanging sleeve and pin it to the back of the quilt. Cut and join sufficient 2"-wide straight strips for a double binding, and bind the edges to complete. (See pages 18 and 19 for more information.)

Label and enjoy!

What should you do with all those leftover squares? Make a scrap quilt!

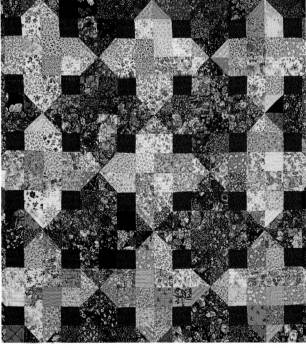

Scrap quilt (detail) made with 2½" squares arranged by value, 48" x 60", 1998.

Drunkard's Trellis, 40" x 56", 1998

Hydrangea Fence, 42" x 46", 2000. Photo by Peter West

Hydrangea Fence

Hydrangea Fence, the cover quilt, is a favorite of mine because of its colors and associations. In the small village of Sychdyn in North Wales where I live, there is always a lovely display of hydrangeas at the end of summer. While enthusing about the colors, it came as no surprise when I was told that the Welsh for hydrangea, "tri lliw ar ddeg," translates literally as "three colors on ten." As I walk past the tidy village gardens, it is that

Pattern for *Hydrangea Fence*. Enlarge by 579%.

variety of color within one flower head and from plant to plant that constantly delights and amazes me. So much so that walking past last year, I felt a quilt coming on! I wanted to be more painterly in my approach to picture making, and this quilt shows the way I have developed the construction of the background picture. I used a larger square ($3\frac{1}{4}$"), which was made up of strips of varying widths, using dyed cottons, batiks, and leafy prints. This method is outlined in Project 6.

Author's Gallery of Gates

Cheltenham Gate, 32" x 49", 1996

Autumn Gate, 38" x 39", 2001

Still Waters, 35" x 36", 1999

Winter Gate, 31" x 33", 2001

Hoffman Gate, 40" x 30", 1999

Summer Gate, 40" x 42", 2001

Grand Slam 10 of Hearts, 23" x 35", 1998

Students' Gallery of Gates

Eaton Gate, 72" x 72", Liz Pedley, Drury, Flintshire, Wales, 2000. Photo by Peter West

Loretta's Gate, 35" x 47", Loretta Bailey, Bretton, Cheshire, England, 1998. Designed by Dilys Fronks

Margaret's Gate, 29" x 35", Margaret Robson, Lower Heswall, Wirral, England, 2000

Summer Garden, 26" x 30", Janet Jones, Ruthin, Denbighshire, Wales, 2000

Our Garden Gate, 27" x 35", Audrey Foster, Heswall, Wirral, England, 2000

Julie's Gate, 26" x 32", Julie Scoffield, Prestatyn, Denbighshire, Wales, 2001

Kath's Gate, 24" x 32", Kath Lloyd, Drury, Flintshire, Wales, 2000

Cat on a Gate, 30" x 40", Connie Evans, Upton, Cheshire, England, 2000

Liberty Gate, 16" x 23", Janet Parry, Prestatyn, Denbighshire, Wales, 2001

Mackintosh Metal, 24" x 30", Mary Williams, Bomere Heath, Cheshire, England, 2001. Designed by Janet Parry

Little Gate, 29" x 36", Liz Pedley, Drury, Flintshire, Wales, 1998

Echoes of Erddig, 33" x 41", Pip Sumbler, Culcheth, Cheshire, England, 1999

Bibliography

Campbell, Marian, *Decorative Ironwork*. London: Victoria and Albert Museum, 1997.

Chatwin, Amina, "Cheltenham's Ornamental Ironwork," self-published with Adprint Ltd., Cheltenham, 1974.

Field, Robert, *Geometric Patterns from Churches and Cathedrals*. Norfolk: Tarquin Publications, 1996.

Hayman, Richard, *Wrought Iron*. Buckinghamshire: Shire Publications Ltd., 2000.

Magaret, Patricia, and Donna Slusser, *Watercolor Imperssions*. Woodinville, WA: Martingale & Company, 1995.

Perry, Gai, *Impressionist Palette*. Lafayette, CA: C&T Publishing, 1997.

Author's Postscript

It has been a pleasure to share my work with you. While working on this book, I often found it difficult to walk past all the fabrics that I desperately wanted to fondle. It was equally hard to ignore a quilt that I dearly wanted to sew in order to sit in front of a computer—a beast with a mind of its own, at least when I come to use it.

"Where has it put that file I was working on yesterday?"

"It's gone and deleted all of section 4!"

"You know that button I shouldn't have pressed? Well, it did exactly what you said it would do!"

"It keeps accusing me of performing an illegal function."

And yet, with the help of Roger, the beast was tamed sufficiently to perform great feats and produce my manuscript, which has been skillfully modeled into this book by the magic of the team at C&T. And so the technology fix is over for the time being. It is with a cheery heart and enthusiastic spirit that I withdraw from the cold, inhospitable feel of the keyboard and the fixed stare of the gray screen back into my own warm, tactile world of quilts, quilts, and more quilts.

Index